S0-GQG-891

DE PROPRIETATIBUS LITTERARUM

edenda curat

C. H. VAN SCHOONEVELD

Indiana University

Series Practica, 43

X 6.40
N   EN

RENCONTRES WITH THE INANIMATE IN PROUST'S *RECHERCHE*

by

H. KOPMAN

New Mexico State University

PQ
2631
R63
A826

1971

MOUTON

THE HAGUE · PARIS

OHIO UNIVERSITY
LIBRARY

© Copyright 1971 in The Netherlands.
Mouton & Co. N.V., Publishers, The Hague.

*No part of this book may be translated or reproduced in any form, by print,
photoprint, microfilm, or any other means, without written permission from the
publishers.*

LIBRARY OF CONGRESS CATALOG CARD NUMBER: 70—169998

Printed in Hungary

PREFACE

This short study will treat of Proust's narrator's chance meetings with all forms of the inanimate (sounds of music; cries of Parisian street vendors; odors and perfumes; sights of trees, blossoms, and cliffs; books; and uneven paving-stones). Needless to say, their rôle in arousing involuntary memory and in evoking the artistic vocation will be discussed.

We feel, though, that those encounters or "rencontres" with nature are the most rewarding. Nature, along with a descriptive writing that is never superfluous nor incidental, makes for us the greatest attraction of all of *A la Recherche du Temps perdu*. Besides reflecting sheer beauty, it is linked with encounters of people, presents an encounter within itself, or is replete with symbols—not necessarily openly expressed by Proust. Rencontres as reminiscences or impressions have brought us a nature where Proust has found "cette relation intime avec la réalité grâce à laquelle l'individu trouve le bonheur".[1] This is, indeed, a dazzling, shimmering, and intimate relation with reality, be it in the sky of Balbec, on the sea, with plants, with varying terrain, or in the haze of a forest in the region of Beauce. In the quotation above one can find a definition of nature and its significance to Proust: a force that is revelation and a phenomenon the brilliant reality of which has brought him closer to happiness, all the while giving the reader a new approach to and picture of the world about us.

[1] Germaine Brée, *Du Temps perdu au Temps retrouvé*, p. 246.

Clearly, Proust does not claim that his experiences with nature were outright mystical in character. He merely poetizes and re-creates. It is up to the individual reader to interpret, to go to the extreme length of seeing possible signs of metempsychosis in the beckoning of shimmering leaves! Proust saw them as beautiful *appels* to an artistic vocation and gave them back to us in an enriched vision.

While Proust's scarcely corresponded to the nineteenth century Romanticist's idea of consolation, it did bring about an atmosphere of the exhilaration, zest, or lure we also feel in some of the other greater descriptive passages in French literature; Chateaubriand striding through the wind-swept reeds and other semi-aquatic plants on the Combourg estate; Saint–Exupéry impressed by the ochre and reddish desert rocks and sand below, the very inanimation of which is animated; Balzac's Félix de Vandenesse viewing the plants of Touraine; a Chactas, begging his beloved Lopez to render him his more-beloved wilderness beyond the distant *cime* of the forest; of Senancour's Obermann exulting in scaling great heights. Here is a force of sensitivity experienced by Sartres's Roquentin upon hearing at Bouville-LeHavre the song, *Some of These Days*, or by many of us who react strongly to certain train-whistles, dove calls, or night jasmine. Proust's treatments of plants and weather, for example, will always attract nature lovers, be they romantic, scientific, contemplative, active and athletic, farmers with souls, aesthetes, or otherwise.

This booklet treating of Proust's rencontres with the inanimate (objects of nature, natural forces–such as the vibrational force known as sound–churches, or perfumes) is the development of the longest chapter of an earlier study of *The Phenomenon of Rencontre in A LA RECHERCHE DU TEMPS PERDU*.

Rencontre as translated by English 'meeting', 'encounter' (but not as 'combat'), or 'chance encounter' was the subject of the above-mentioned study. Giving a brief analysis of *The Phenomenon of Rencontre in A LA RECHERCHE DU TEMPS PERDU* will facilitate a better understanding of the more limited subject of this booklet and will serve to put rencontre with the inanimate (particularly with the beauties of nature) in its proper place within the cadre of encounter in general.

Here, then, is an abstract of the original and longer study: *Rencontres*, as they occurred throughout Marcel Proust's vast novel, were both tabulated and analysed as aesthetic phenomena. Rencontre's meaning was extended to include falling upon inanimate objects. On occasion the term was used in reference to human and artistic elements; for example, recognition of the conjuncture of specific human beings and works of art: a picture that resembles a person, persons whose appearances evoke artistic works (the kitchen-girl at Combray and Bellini's *Charité*). Nowhere did *rencontre* signify 'hostile meeting'.

In *La Recherche* Proust's narrator had the most important rencontres. 'Chance encounters' with people, phenomena obviously indispensable to plot development, were less important than rencontres with inanimate objects. These latter encounters stimulated involuntary memory, sometimes known as authentic memory, helped the Narrator discover the artistic vocation. Rencontre, then, could mean self-encounter or self-realization.

The Narrator's self-realization, along with the story of Proust's other characters, was traced in terms of rencontre in four areas; love, inanimate objects (especially in Nature), society, and art.

Love rencontre was treated in seven divisions: Swann's story, Marcel's imagined or abortive love encounters and episodes with Gilberte, Oriane, and Albertine, Saint-Loup's affair with Rachel, Charlus' unusual activities, and family-love and friendship. In *rencontre souhaitée* or *désirée* (hoped-for encounter with a known person or one imagined and idealized) often no actual meeting developed. The same obtains for the Proustian pattern of *rencontre manquée* (missed rendez-vous or abortive love encounters). Two results of love encounters were arousal of artistic sensitivity through sensuality and the learning or recognition of suffering's value to the eventual artist. Love rencontre, then, could mean revelation.

Marcel's fullest revelation came about from rencontres with inanimate objects. Dozens of such meetings were tabulated and

analyzed within two categories: reminiscences (such as the celebrated *madeleine* experience or the Narrator's chancing upon *pavés
inégaux* in *Le Temps retrouvé)* or impressions (such as the hawthorn
experience in "Combray"). Impressions, as experiences, gave Marcel
hints of his intended vocation, writing, whereas certain reminiscences discovered for him his literary calling in remarkable experiences
of involuntary memory. Such *rencontres* were natural vehicles for
themes: (1) chance opposed to necessity, (2) mobility and immobility as aesthetic-ethical ideas, (3) artistic vocation, (4) sheer
joy, (5) filigrane plot development, (6) natural beauty and appeal–
often presented metaphorically, (7) *La Recherche's* time-effacing
value. A *vocation* sprang from *appeals*, themselves *chance* sensations
resulting from fortuitous encounters with *natural objects* (and
differing weather, sights, smells, and sounds).

Social rencontres, between individuals, groups, or individuals
and groups, were fecund for Proust's narrator. They helped him
attain some reality, conceive an idea of evolving French society
amidst Time laws, find material for his literary work.

Rencontres with art and artists (Elstir, Vinteuil, Bergotte), while
not startling revelations as were the experiences with nature, did
further Marcel's quest for a vocation. Rich encounters with churches
or statues presenting a conjuncture of the human and the artistic
symbolized temporal permanence. The Elstir meeting was a pre-
figuration of the Narrator's self-encounter or self-realization.
Vinteuil's music showed art as the only true rencontre as communion
of souls.

Rencontre patterns showed: (1) the interplay of chance and
necessity, (2) expanding, "snow-ball" meetings in a web-filigrane
plot, (3) interweaving of themes, as love with nature, inanimate
objects with art, (4) orderly, connected encounters throughout
La Recherche. In an appendix this formula of symmetry, tinged
with occasional ambiguities, is compared with rencontre patterns
of nineteen other modern French novelists.

Proust's rencontres have advanced literary pattern while rev-
ealing a play of change and chance within a determined framework.
More important, encounter was revelation of temporal permanence.

Poetic, if not mystical, rencontres signalized a lasting essence in both man and nature.

Now it is time to examine Proust's brilliant treatment of the inanimate, especially of nature.

TABLE OF CONTENTS

Preface 5

1. The Appeal of Such Experiences 13

2. Distinctive Types of Experience 17

3. Striking Rencontres as Reminiscences 20

4. Striking Impressions and Descriptions 60

5. Conclusion 75

Bibliography 81

Index 83

1

THE APPEAL OF SUCH EXPERIENCES

> Il y aurait toute une étude, et passionnante et fructueuse à faire, sur les résonances qu'éveille dans l'âme de Marcel Proust la vue d'un tableau, le goût d'une madeleine, ou la forme du nez du cocher Remi, sur les prolongements déroulés en tous sens qui vont frapper, saisir, insoucieux du temps, de l'espace, dans le monde des idées, des hommes, des arts, ou de la vie intérieure tout ce qui peut constituer, avec l'émotion actuelle, avec l'objet, souvent insignifiant lui-même de cette émotion, et qui ne doit son prix qu'à sa vertu de centre d'attraction, un merveilleux bouquet.
>
> Louis Martin-Chauffier in *Les Cahiers Marcel Proust* I

Proust, attaining the acme of both sensitivity and style, throws into relief the rôle of recurrent sounds, feelings, smells, and sights and their associative values. These are, indeed, *rencontres* within themselves. This rich realm, though not entirely overlooked by the best French novelists, had not been explored before. For those particularly sensitive to such phenomena, there is delight in reading passages in Proust's novel which vary from gracious descriptions of meetings with hawthorns to the unusual treatment of the aural sensation stimulated by the water-pipe sound in *Le Temps retrouvé*.

Some readers are inclined to appreciate especially this aspect of Proust's work because the celebrated rencontres with inanimate objects inciting involuntary memory evoke a happy world of eternity and optimism,[1] whereas the world of rencontres with people has been marked with disillusionment, the ravages of physical time, and a pronounced pessimism. Perhaps the very force of this world of things lies, not in that it fosters isolation and escape from the world of humans, but rather in its eventual power to link the two spheres, human and inanimate. According to Daniel-Rops, one of the merits of Georges Cattaui, in touching upon this aspect of Proust's work, "est de montrer que les deux aspects ne sont en rien séparés, qu'ils constituent les deux volets d'un dyptique où s'exprime... une même recherche." Nor is the world of things truly inanimate for Proust, who goes beyond the mere picture or smell in an attempt to capture the "essence" of things and their intimate relation to the *moi*.

Whereas there are tedious passages at times in the novel, one senses, by the very absence of such passages in these descriptions of rencontres with objects, Proust's intensity of feeling and intellectual conviction when dealing with this capital theme.

This intensity of conviction stems from no ordinary observation and reproduction of reality but, rather, from Proust's unusual power of contemplation and 're-creation' as it has been called by some critics. Proust seems to have enjoyed moments of 'total awareness' which resulted in evocations that transcend objective descriptions of the Flaubertian type. One critic describes this particular power of Marcel Proust as follows:

Ainsi qu'il l'a confessé, il ne savait pas observer, regarder autour de lui, selon l'acceptation que l'on donne d'ordinaire à ces mots. La vue des êtres ou des choses le plongeait dans une sorte d'hébétude, de transe, où se révélaient non leurs petites caractéristiques accidentelles, mais leur essence la plus intime, si bien que l'on pouvait dire de lui ce qu'on a dit de Goethe qu'il était un mystique voué à la contemplation de l'extériorité. En ces états de l'âme presque surnaturels, dont parle Baudelaire, "la profondeur de la vie se révèle tout entière dans le spectacle, si ordinaire qu'il soit, qu'on a sous les yeux. Il en devient le symbole."[2]

[1] Harold March, *The Two Worlds of Marcel Proust*, p. 146.
[2] Georges Cattaui, *Marcel Proust*, p. 192.

These moments of revelation seem always, in the case of Proust, to arise from the contemplation of natural beauty in land- or seascape.

Moreover, this aspect of Proust's writing is particularly impelling in that it reveals a vital feeling for nature. Among literary figures and natural scientists profoundly appreciative of the objects and phenomena of this earth, there is a common essence and a similarly shared vibrant response to such beauty. Appreciation of this sort is not confined to breathtaking scenery. Such perception does not require lovely Switzerland and her "declamatory landscape"[3] as an object and source of admiration. Genuine veneration of nature, in the case of truly responsive persons, can be inspired just as easily by the gnarled cedars and oaks on the limestone cliffs of the American Ozarks, certainly not a high and awe-inspiring range.

Proust, so little travelled, was satisfied with the landscape of northern and central France, drawing chiefly upon the limited areas of Illiers and the Channel coast. This particular natural setting is hardly 'declamatory'. We label it, rather, as 'domesticated'. It is a *paysage moyen*.[4] As DuBellay discovered a "douceur angevine", Proust was responsive to a "douceur beauceronne" or "normande". He appreciated homely and quiet scenes, limiting himself to simple and humble things.[5][6] He and his narrator would contemplate with fervour forest haze, or the play of light on a mere stone or roof, or some common flower, all in an unpretentious setting (I, 150, 167 and 178).[7]

What characterizes Proust's evocations and distinguishes him from among his many predecessors, is that he attempted to explain

[3]   Thus termed, ever so pejoratively, in *Les Faux-Monnayeurs*.
[4]   A term employed by Laumonier in explaining Ronsard's appreciation of Vendôme.
[5]   Georges Cattaui, *Marcel Proust*, p. 187; or III, 623; or I, 49; or André Maurois, *A la Recherche de Marcel Proust*, p. 330.
[6]   For note '5' there are no fewer than two Proustian textual references and two critical references, for "les choses les plus humbles" is a phrase much used by Proust and his critics.
[7]   All textual references are to the 3-volume "Pléiade" edition of *A la Recherche du Temps perdu*.

how and why certain plants, landscapes, or effects of light are beautiful for the Narrator. Proust's narrator shares with his author a feeling that at times shimmering leaves or the blossoms of fruit trees are beckoning to him; and Proust felt that plants and landscapes may, indeed, be sending us a message. It is clear that he was acutely sensitive to beautiful objects and desirous of conveying to us the significance they held for him.

In *A la Recherche du Temps perdu* descriptions of natural objects, rencontres with them, and the messages they may harbour appeal to many readers because of their optimistic character and their role in linking the worlds of characters and things. Their stylistic presentation is unique. In them the crystallization of Proust's mystical contemplation becomes evident. In them is the stamp of a profound veneration of Nature, not merely the lore of a professional naturalist.[8]

In fact, Proust, other than calling plants by their proper names, never writes of nature in a learned or scientific fashion–this in spite of his avowed excellence as a young student of natural history. Nor does he refer frequently to animals. Sometimes he alludes vaguely to a 'bird', rarely identifying exactly. *Corbeau, mésange bleue, hirondelle, martinet* are some of the exceptions. It is interesting to note, further, that to the much-treated plant-life, animal-life, as we said, takes a subsidiary position, what with only casual references, or even metaphorical allusions, to tadpoles, an isolated crow, a flight of crows (perhaps mistaken once for *choucas*), to a "butterfly" that might be flying over the water, and to flies, a 'salamander', a wasp, or the carp. He also writes of the *coucou*, but a common bird, especially in forested Northern France.

DISTINCTIVE TYPES OF EXPERIENCE

Marcel Proust was careful to distinguish between *réminiscences* and *impressions*. In fact, his various experiences with objects or forces of nature may well be divided into as many as five types:

(1) the veritable reminiscences, such as the incidents of the *madeleine*, of the *pavés inégaux*, of the *serviette*, which are the celebrated "moments identiques" and pivotal points within the novel;

(2) the so-called *impressions bienheureuses*–such as the rencontres with the hawthorns or the *clochers de Martinville*, which are *appels*, and, like the first category, privileged, if not identical moments;

(3) the rencontre with the three trees, which seems to be a fusion of the first two types; for a genuine *réminiscence* is not involved, but rather a hint at metempsychosis; thus it is an *appel* and a suggestion of some form of reincarnation:

Die Bäume beschwören die Seele wie die Phantome einer Vorzeit, wie die Schatten entschwundener Freunde: 'Nimm uns und gib uns dem Leben wieder.'[1]

(4) the rencontre, here and there within the novel, with a beautiful scene; for instance, the narrator's first view of the sea, which gives rise to pure description rather than to direct allusions to the hidden *appel* or *réminiscence;*

(5) those rencontres with sights or sounds that, again, give rise not to an *appel* nor to a *réminiscence* but to a description which

---

[1] Robert Curtius, *Französischer Geist im zwanzigsten Jahrhundert*, p. 287.

is this time a metaphor, as seen in the following example, an Elstir-like rendition of light through sound:

Il faisait à peine assez clair pour lire, et la sensation de la splendeur de la lumière ne m'était donnée que par les coups frappés dans la rue... qui, retentissant dans l'atmosphère sonore, spéciale aux temps chauds, semblaient faire voler au loin des astres écarlates; et aussi par les mouches qui exécutaient devant moi, dans leur petit concert, comme la musique de chambre de l'été.[2]

All five of these categories of experiences are related. The first and fifth classifications are each in a distinct way, *correspondances–rapports* between points in time as seen in the first, and *rapport* in sensations as exhibited in the fifth. Each category, too, involves a certain appeal. Similarly, the common role of association is evident in several, if not all, types of rencontre. We have only to think of the combination memories of Balbec-*serviette* (III, 868; which we have just given as an example under the category '1', veritable *réminiscences*), or the aggregate 'hawthorns-Combray-Catholic' in the renowned impression-rencontre to which we have alluded under category '2', and, finally, that most unusual assemblage and association of summer light, air, flies, and packing-case crowbars alluded to in the passage just quoted.

This particular phenomenon of associative values appears at a very early point in the novel. In the scene known as the "drame du coucher", the first episode in the novel, hypersensitive Marcel was obliged to go up to bed deprived of his mother's good-night kiss. As he went up the stairway, his susceptible nose caught the distinctive odor of banister varnish. This smell, for the rest of his days, was to be associated with his despair and childish lamentations on that particular evening.

This special kind of association that links things and sentiments or things and people, a particular type of *association* that is neither a reminiscence nor an impression, can give rise to even a sixth category of expression, as indicated in three specific examples: (1) early in the novel (I, 145), a puff of wind which the narrator

[2] I, p. 83.

feels has passed by Gilberte before reaching him reminded him of the idealized little girl he had seen as he walked over the plain Méséglise-Way; (2) in *A l'Ombre des jeunes filles en fleurs* (I, 503), Madame Swann's perfume seemed to arouse for Marcel the charm not only of Gilberte but of all things surrounding her; (3) Marcel, returning home one evening, during that epoch of his life when Albertine was his virtual prisoner, saw a streaked light on the window of the room she was occupying, an image not merely associated with Albertine but also a symbol of their concurrent imprisonment in their odd love-affair. These examples might fall, then, into a possible sixth classification.

Such detailed codifying or labelling of rencontres could be endless. For example, Léon Guichard in *Introduction à la lecture de Proust* distinguishes between direct and indirect *appels* and between encounters encouraging or discouraging. For the practical purposes of our review of these assorted yet similar types of rencontre, we shall use merely the two-fold classification of reminiscences and impressions, keeping in mind, however, the five – or even six – shades of difference listed above.

STRIKING RENCONTRES AS REMINISCENCES

The more important rencontres that bear upon the novel's chief message are the reminiscences which bring into play involuntary memory. One finds the key ones in the "matinée chez les Guermantes" episode of *Le Temps retrouvé*. There Proust grouped the capital rencontres that capture the *moi*, dominate time, and reveal to the narrator his artistic vocation. They are thus the culmination of the whole novel's descriptive passages of *impressions*, which will be considered later.

Here, then, in quick succession, are the reminiscences to which we referred in the above paragraph: (1) Marcel had a re-encounter with the name, Guermantes, (III, 856) in the form of an invitation to the "matinée chez la princesse de Guermantes"; (2) the touching of the paving stones in the Guermantes' courtyard reminded the narrator of the uneven stones before St. Mark's of Venice (III, 867); (3) the sound of a spoon against a plate evoked a stopped train and a hammerstroke upon its wheel (III, 868); (4) the touch of a starched napkin made Marcel recall Balbec (III, 868); (5) the sound of water in a pipe was remindful of the boats off Balbec (III, 874); (6) finally, a chance encounter with the book, *François le Champi*, recalled for the narrator the first episode of the novel, the "drame du coucher" to which we have just alluded.

The well-known incident of the *pavés inégaux* and the incidents related to it which follow are, in a sense, the consummation of Proust's novel; but rencontres found earlier in the novel and hinting at this same experience prepare its climax. From "Combray" to *Le Temps retrouvé* there is, if not a circle, something of a connecting arch of such incidents. We cannot term this arc a rainbow, for it has instead of the several color channels that represent all the colors of the spectrum, only two channels. They are equivalent to alternating electrical circuits and are concerned with what we might term "electrical coincidences". They lead in reverse directions from the two extremes of *La Recherche*. These rencontres extend from the celebrated *madeleine* incident to the Guermantes matinée and back again. They are numerous and varied, as a systematic tabular presentation of these *rencontres* — reminiscences will show.

We propose, therefore:

A. to list by categories and in tabular form all the important rencontres in this vast novel.

B. to show, by developing and analyzing a few outstanding rencontres in volumes of *La Recherche* before *Le Temps* retrouvé, how these classified encounters (1) have symbolistic significance, (2) show with what sense of balance and symmetry Proust constructed his seemingly formless novel, (3) link humans and things.

C. to show how the rencontres in *Le Temps retrouvé* are related to the significance of the novel as a whole.

These classifications of rencontres we list as follows:

Rencontres with:

(1) trees, shrubs, and their blossoms,

(2) weather, especially changing weather that serves to combat the paralyzing effects of Habit,

(3) sounds, including those harmonious sounds of music,

(4) odors,

(5) names, particularly those of Guermantes, Gilberte, and Swann,

(6) places, particularly of the Combray area, the Guermantes property, and Tansonville,

(7) inanimate objects definitely associated with characters of the novel.

Besides these, there are also, of undisputed importance recontres:

(8) that evoke the artistic vocation, particularly in *Le Temps retrouvé*,

(9) that (similar to those of category "8") hint (earlier in the novel) at the artistic vocation.

Finally, of necessity, there are encounters:

(10) within a group entitled "miscellaneous", for there are in the *Recherche* some *rencontres* that defy strict classification.

Now, before making an analysis of individual encounters and a synthesis of the above-listed categories of rencontres, we proceed to a tabular presentation of the rencontres with the inanimate in the *Recherche*.

(1) RENCONTRES WITH TREES, SHRUBS, AND THEIR BLOSSOMS:

I, 111: The first re-encounter with the hawthorns, which is the narrator's almost over-sensitive *adieu* to the hawthorns of Tansonville before his return to Paris. The narrator's initial encounters with them had been in their cut-state in the church of Combray (I, 112) and in their natural state while he was walking Méséglise-Way (I, 138). These preliminary rencontres had been impressions and not reminiscences.

I, 153: The first re-encounter with the lilacs, wherein Proust tells us how the narrator heard "les derniers roulements du tonnerre roucouler dans les lilas". The narrator's initial rencontre had been presented in the lengthy and beautiful description of a walk Méséglise-Way (I, 135).

I, 182: The first re-encounter with the apple-trees, as the narrator returned to his aunt's house at Combray after the long walk Guermantes-Way. The narrator's initial encounter, Méséglise-Way, had served to impress upon him the inimitable leaf-shape of and the sort of shadow cast by this particular type of fruit tree.

I, 707: An apple-tree branch bought in Paris served to revive memories of Balbec.

I, 717–19: The celebrated encounter with the 'three trees'. The narrator while riding with Madame de Villeparisis had met with three trees that seemed to beckon to him. If this was not an actual re-encounter, it was at least a partial reminiscence; for here there is hinting at a form of metempsychosis.

I, 922: A further rencontre with hawthorns: This occurred towards the end of *A l'Ombre des jeunes filles en fleurs*. Marcel had stumbled upon them near Balbec while searching for the cliffs of Creunier.

II, 160 :A further rencontre with fruit-trees: While with Saint-Loup and his mistress, Rachel, at a Parisian suburb, the narrator found again a definite *appel* in nearby pear- and cherry-trees in blossom. (We note with interest that he had, a few pages previously (II, 155), referred to a group of *three* pear-trees in this suburban setting. We shall see how this particular number, three, plays a particular role in both his reminiscences and impressions.)

II, 384: A rencontre with "des peupliers tremblants qui rappellent les mystères du soir plus qu'ils n'y répondent" while the narrator is strolling around the Bois de Boulogne, very much pre-occupied with Madame de Stermaria. The first encounter with the *peuplier* had also been in autumn when Marcel perceived "le peuplier de la rue des Perchamps adresser à l'orage des supplications et des salutations désespérées." (I, 152).

II, 781: This is a rencontre with fruit trees described in an atmosphere impregnated with Marcel's prolonged despair over his grand-mother's death and with his embryonic affair with Albertine. It could also be listed with encounters with changing weather; for here was a spring day, one that started warm, displayed apple blossoms and that delightful little bird, *la mésange bleue*, and finished in a chill rain – but with the apple trees ever erect in their flowery, pink beauty.

III, 175: A further rencontre with trees in the Bois de Boulogne which again tried to render a message. These trees were the cadre of an idyllic scene with Albertine: "où les arbres d'hiver, habillés de lierre et de ronce, comme des ruines, semblaient conduire à la demeure d'un magicien".

III, 697: At Tansonville, Marcel experienced only mediocre pleasure in re-viewing the lilacs and forest trees.

III, 855: Trees viewed from a stopped train were even less inspiring than were those of the above-listed rencontre. The narrator is now confronted with discouragement rather than an *appel* to *"la* seule vérité" and the artistic vocation.

(2) RENCONTRES WITH CHANGING WEATHER

I, 405: In a mystical atmosphere of unseasonable weather, as felt in a description of spring in winter, of pre-spring, we feel the full force of the *rencontre rêvée,* be it that of Gilberte or that of Balbec.

I, 634: In a reverse situation, winter reappears in spring, with a suddenly recurring and clinging cold. We are reminded that "l'hiver, le printemps, l'été ne sont pas séparés par des cloisons aussi hermétiques que tend à le croire le boulevardier". It is not only the reverse of the above situation but also an excellent example of Proustian contrast-equilibrium in that it is associated with the waning rather than the budding of Marcel's love for Gilberte.

II, 345: A suddenly occurring fog is effective as an *appel,* for "un changement de temps suffit à recréer le monde et nous-mêmes" and "le monde nouveau dans lequel le brouillard de ce matin m'avait plongé était un monde déjà connu de moi."

III, 11: Suddenly appearing sunlight, the reverse of the above situation, can equally well break the anesthetizing power of Habit: "Le soleil tout à coup jaunissait cette mousseline de verre, la dorait et, découvrant doucement en moi un jeune homme plus ancien qu'avait caché l'habitude, me grisait de souvenirs."

III, 880: In a "béquet", in which light and sound are linked as in so many of Proust's impressionistic passages, the sudden *bourdonnement* of sunlight against a curtain makes the narrator think again of things long forgotten.

(3) SOUNDS, INCLUDING MUSIC, AS RENCONTRES

I: The *"petite phrase"*[1] of Vinteuil, that recurring bit of music so well-known to readers of Proust, is analyzed particularly on the following pages of Volume I: 208–212, 218–19, 236–37,

---

[1]   Admittedly, sounds, including those of music, are not *objects,* but they are inanimate *forces* and can be included in this chapter.

353–54, and 533. (In Chapter I[2], which is entitled "The Rencontre in Love", the *petite phrase* in *La Recherche*" has been discussed. Its artistic significance to both Swann and the narrator will be mentioned later in this particular booklet.)

II, 120: Puffs of wind, reminding the narrator of both Gilberte and Madame de Guermantes are linked nicely in the following: "Un souffle d'air un peu doux qui passait, semblait m'apporter un message d'elle (Madame de Guermantes), comme jadis de Gilberte dans les blés de Méséglise." (cf. I, 145).

II, 347: The sound of a furnace will evoke memories:

Depuis le matin on avait allumé le nouveau calorifère à eau. Son bruit désagréable, qui poussait de temps à autre une sorte de hoquet, n'avait aucun rapport avec mes souvenirs de Doncières. Mais sa rencontre prolongée avec eux en moi, cet après-midi, allait lui faire contracter avec eux telle affinité que, chaque fois que (un peu déshabitué de lui) j'entendrais de nouveau le chauffage central, il me les rappellerait.

III, 253: The music of Vinteuil is described on this page as what we might term a "lieu de rencontre"[3]; it is described on page 258, III, as a means of communication of souls; and, again, on pages 373 and 374, III, it is termed an important vehicle for encounter.

III, 375: The rencontre with Vinteuil's music is compared favorably with that of the *clochers de Martinville* or the *madeleine* experience; yet, a few pages on, it (III, 382) is analyzed as a somewhat discouraging element in the narrator's experience, having produced nothing more than a consciousness of *le néant*.

III, 868: In *Le Temps retrouvé*, the sound of a spoon striking against a dish summoned forth the noise of a hammer against a wheel of a halted train.

III, 874: A water-pipe sound invited the memory to reproduce the whistling of boats off Balbec.

[2]   I. e., Chapter I of H., Kopman, *The Phenomenon of Rencontre in A La Recherche du Temps perdu.*
[3]   Expression used effectively by Germaine Brée in *Du Temps perdu au Temps retrouvé*, pages 53 and 67.

III, 1056: At the very end of the novel there is a re-encounter within the depth of the soul with the compelling little bell of Combray, a *sonnette* that induced one to produce a work of art based upon a recaptured past.

(4) ODORS

I, 28: We are made very conscious of odors and their associative values early in "Combray". We have mentioned the narrator's telling us at that point of the novel that he would always link the smell of a varnished stairway with his unhappy boyhood evenings. As he would climb the stairs, he would sniff the varnish, and, at the same time, give vent to boyhood lamentations over his being cut off from his mother for the evening.

I, 41: the odor of the *madeleine* as well as its taste.

I, 492: The moldy odor in a small *"pavillon"* reminded Marcel of the "petit cabinet sentant l'iris" at Combray. (I, 12).

I, 503: Here is a reference to the scent, so fragrant, of the perfume of Madame Swann. It served Marcel as a link to the general charm of Gilberte and to everyone and everything surrounding her.

III, 26: The odor of burning twigs in a Parisian setting recalled the rooms of Doncières and Combray.

III, 411: A spring morning's odors in Paris evoked the "odeurs naturelles" (of dried fruits, fruit preserves, etc.) of Combray (I, 49).

III, 412: As disagreeable and meaningless as it might be for some, automobile oil summons forth for Marcel poppies and cornflowers of Normandy.

III, 919: Finally, there is an important reference to reminiscence and odor ("Odeur fine et suave d'héliotrope") in Chateaubriand's *Mémoires d'Outre-Tombe*. This is found in a passage discussing the aesthetic procedures of Chateaubriand, Gérard de Nerval, and Baudelaire.

(5) NAMES

I, 361: By a rather indirect association of the names Beuzeval, Beuzeville, and Bréauté, Swann's jealousy is revived.

I, 388: Though we are perhaps more concerned with the names of persons, it is interesting to note still another example of the role of the place-name early in the novel: When the name of Parma was repeated, it had for the narrator all the charm of Stendhal's *Chartreuse*.

I, 394: Marcel, one day, playing on a lawn just off the Champs-Elysées, heard Gilberte's name called out. He and we (the readers) are at once reminded of an equally magical encounter with a name earlier in the novel: In a stroll Swann's Way, Marcel had heard Gilberte's name called out, "donné comme un talisman qui me permettrait peut-être de retrouver un jour celle dont il venait de faire une personne et qui, l'instant d'avant n'était qu'une image incertaine". (I, 141–2).

I, 413: As the narrator felt the fascination and growing rapture of his love for Gilberte, he referred to "Ce nom, devenu pour moi presque mythologique, de Swann." (I, 144). Towards the end of *Du Côté de chez Swann* (I, 413), the narrator experienced the thrill of "un nom nouveau" upon hearing anyone utter the name of Swann.

II, 12: If, by some play of chance, the narrator heard the name of Guermantes called out, he would recall his first rencontre with Madame de Guermantes (I, 174) at the marriage of Mademoiselle de Percepied in the Combray church; and, indeed, when he later hears the name he "breathes the air of Combray of that particular year." (II, 12).

III, 856: In *Le Temps retrouvé*, the name of Guermantes in the invitation to the *matinée* which terminates the novel is surely the name-encounter of primary importance. We could have listed the chance meeting with the title of a book (that of *François le Champi*, listed elsewhere in this chapter); we could have listed a goodly number of rencontres (surely most familiar to even the causal reader of *La Recherche*) with placenames, as Venice or Balbec (I, 384; I, 386, etc.); but the encounter with the name of Guermantes (III, 856) is certainly the most meaningful of all – as we shall see.

(6) PLACES (PARTICULARLY OF THE COMBRAY AREA)

I, 62: This passage at this particular point, although not an example of actual reminiscence, fortells significant rencontres: those with the little church of Combray and those with other churches.

I,   659: The rencontre with Balbec and her church: One notes preparation for this encounter in "Noms de Pays", Chapter III of *Du Côté de chez Swann*, in a passage of *rencontre rêvée*.

I,   705: At this point we are told that the sea is always different, thus forever a rich rencontre: Proust's protagonist views the sea under different conditions from the hotel at Balbec. Such *tableaux* are at the same time reminiscences and impressions.

II,   384: Here, and on the following pages, is a renewed acquaintance and lyrical description of Marcel's Bois de Boulogne, "ce royaume romanesque des rencontres" – where he is hoping to meet Madame de Stermaria.

III,   651: The re-search for a street encountered the evening before in Venice is compared to the *rencontre rêvée* or *souhaitée* of a woman.

III, 691–692: The *deuxième rencontre* with Tansonville has left the older Marcel most indifferent and discouraged.

III,   858: On the way to the Guermantes' *matinée*, the narrator took streets over which he had formerly walked with Françoise when going to the Champs-Elysées. They did not exact the effort of adaptation and attention required when one is confronted with *"les choses nouvelles"*.

(7) INANIMATE OBJECTS ASSOCIATED WITH THE NOVEL'S CHARACTERS

I, 145 and
II,   120: (We have already mentioned, under the category 'rencontres with sounds', the puffs of wind which linked the narrator with both Gilberte and Madame de Guermantes.)

I, 345–347: (We have already mentioned the several encounters with the *petite phrase de Vinteuil*. Swann's connecting this bit of music with his love for Odette (I, 345) at the *soirée chez la Marquise Saint-Euverte* is perhaps the most touching reference to the *morceau*.)

I,   578: Aunt Léonie's furniture was discovered in a brothel. While thinking back upon the 'virtues of Combray', the protagonist felt that the large sofa and other pieces "me semblaient vivre et me supplier, comme ces objects en apparence inanimés d'un conte persan, dans lesquels sont enfermées des âmes qui subissent un martyre et implorent leur délivrance."

II,   79: a chance encounter with Madame de Guermantes' photograph.

II, 755–756: In the celebrated passage on the "intermittences du coeur", Marcel's shoe-buttons and a certain stooping gesture revive memories of his grandmother.

III, 253 and 373: The music[4] of Vinteuil is shown to be a *"lieu de rencontre"*, which links late in the novel Vinteuil, his daughter, Marcel, Morel, Léa, and Albertine.

III, 462: Françoise had found for the narrator rings Albertine had left behind upon fleeing Marcel forever.

III, 481: A moonbeam and a bench remind the narrator of Albertine.

III, 542: Marcel, sleeping in his hotel bed at Balbec, calls it the "cadre de notre amour". (For that matter, any room in *La Recherche* is a vital *"lieu de rencontre".)*

(8) INANIMATE OBJECTS THAT EVOKE THE ARTISTIC VOCATION

 I, 179–182: (The rencontre with the *clochers de Martinville* arouses dedicated artisty in a most forcible manner, but this experience will be discussed fully in Chapter 4 of this booklet since it is something that should be considered more as an impression than as a reminiscence.)

III, 867: Along with the *madeleine* experience, the most widely-discussed encounter in *La Recherche* is that with the *pavés inégaux*.

III, 868–870: Similar rencontres *chez les Guermantes* with a spoon and with a napkin. Both, again, arouse involuntary memory; the former recalls a stopped train, and the latter summons forth Balbec.

III, 874: the shrill and harsh sound of water-pipe vibration – one that recalls Balbec.

---

[4] As we indicated, footnote, p. 24, although music and other sounds are not inanimate *objects*, they are a natural force, a vibrational energy that produces the sensation of hearing; thus inclusion in this listing is justified as sounds are of the realm of 'the inanimate'.

III, 883: The discovery of a copy of *François le Champi*. This is but an extension of the experience that embraces the four preceding rencontres.

(9) INANIMATE OBJECTS RADIATING HINTS AT THE ARTISTIC VOCATION

(This category excludes, naturally, certain celebrated impressions – as the one with the hawthorns in "Combray", I, 138, – which, too, are hints and *appels.)*

I, 178–179: While on walks Guermantes-Way, Marcel would go back to review the play of light on a rock or other phenomena of physical nature which were hinting at his hidden calling even if they did not reveal it directly.

I, 717–719: (Under the classification of trees we have mentioned the meeting with the three trees Hudimesnil Way, again a forcible hint.)

II, 30: At this point in the novel, there is a reference to the possible existence of *"moments identiques"* in life.

II, 1126: Here is another hint of the true realization of Marcel's life: "Deux ou trois fois, pendant un instant, j'eus l'idée que le monde où étaient cette chambre et ces bibliothèques, et dans lequel Albertine était si peu de chose, était peut – être un monde intellectuel, qui était la seule réalité..."

III, 263: A direct reference to the hidden appeal of Vinteuil's music, which is called "l'étrange appel" which "je ne cesserais plus jamais d'entendre comme la promesse qu'il existait autre chose, réalisable dans l'art sans doute..."

(10) MISCELLANEOUS RENCONTRES

I, 114–115: At this early point in the novel, we encounter a very simple and direct allusion to the association of sound, smell, and light that will awaken memory: the barking of dogs, no matter where, will be linked to the perfume of linden (lime) trees and to the play of moonlight – and the *boulevard de la gare de Combray* will appear to the narrator, as much of Combray appeared as if out of the tea-cup of the *madeleine* experience.

II,   83: We note with keen interest that the very sensation of steps is treated hundreds of pages ahead of the eventual treatment of the *pavés inégaux* (which occurs on p. 867, III). Proust, midway in the novel, has given an analysis of this sensation of feeling steps – put on the plane of olfactory, visual, and gustatory experiences.

III,   494: On this page the eyes and voice (certainly not 'inanimate' but certainly not the whole person) of Madame de Guermantes recall Combray for the narrator. We are aware, too, of the fact that inversely, in various parts of the novel, this "sol" along the Vivonne recalled Madame de Guermantes.

III, 284–285: In an unique situation, the narrator is aware of another person's reminiscences: He is conscious of Brichot's reminiscing by way of Madame Verdurin's old furniture.

III,   331: The following may be termed a reminiscence, a symbol, or a metaphor: One evening the narrator viewed the streaked light on Albertine's window while she was his 'guest'. For him this was a symbol of her (and his) imprisonment. Furthermore, it is the almost exact reproduction of Swann's experience (I, 274) of seeing the streaked light on Odette's window in his own imprisoned search for truth.

III, 1040: The accidental appearance of Madame Molé's invitation card reminded the narrator of the all-important conflict of obligations to both the social and artistic worlds.

TREES, SHRUBS, AND THEIR BLOSSOMS

(Analysis of individual rencontres within the category and synthesis of their general significance)

The category, 'trees, shrubs, and their blossoms', which appeared in first position in this listing, produced the greatest number of encounters, and now merits the fullest discussion. The narrator's awareness of plants is a natural consequence of his sensitive early boyhood spent in their midst. Apple-trees and lilac bushes were a familiar, intimate part of what was to prove to be the most meaningful of experiences: remembrance of things attached to one's own life.

Trees, like church towers, are particularly expressive for Proust's protagonist because "Les expériences les plus profondes sont liées à des sensations de l'espace."[5] He responds not only to their linear perspective but also to their upright position.

While Proust was not religious, he was spiritual. Something of what certain people see in the high and noble towers of Reims Cathedral is felt in *La Recherche* through the medium of trees, upright trees whose branches are reared skyward as are the two tower-arms of the celebrated cathedral facing east.

Much of the novel and much of Proust's theme of the artistic vocation are based upon the appeal of natural objects. Nothing could better typify such an *appel* or beckoning than a tree. The very leaves perform such 'gestures'.

Within this meaningful category, the encounter with the "three trees Hudimesnil-Way" first demands our attention. The narrator had been riding with Mme de Villeparisis in her carriage. She was taking him on a tour of the Norman countryside just after showing him the "façade végétale" of a village church. During this latter stop he had just had an inconclusive rencontre with a peasant girl (I, 717). Then, as he and Mme de Villeparisis went on their way towards Hudimesnil, three trees appeared on the horizon. These trees that marked the entrance to a sideroad produced in the narrator a sensation of happiness, as had the towers of Martinville earlier in the novel. Only this time, he was unable to understand their message:

Je regardais les trois arbres, je les voyais bien, mais mon esprit sentait qu'ils recouvraient quelque chose sur quoi il n'avait pas prise, comme sur ces objects placés trop loin dont nos doigts, allongés au bout de notre bras rendu, effleurent seulement par instant l'enveloppe sans arriver à rein saisir.[6]

What was their charm? Marcel asked himself a series of questions: Was this a reminiscence of a boyhood scene? Had he seen the trees in a dream the night before? Was their beckoning appeal so

---

[5]   Georges Cattaui; *op. cit.*, p. 267.
[6]   I, 717.

great that he mistook this experience for a reminiscence? He even hinted at the possibility of metempsychosis.

In any case, spiritual growth and temporal permanence seem to have been typified in this rencontre with three[7] trees, with three *old* trees, when he was in the carriage with Mme de Villeparisis.[8]

Her disturbing presence prevented the encounter with the three trees from being thoroughly fecund. Her being there kept Marcel from analyzing such an experience tranquilly and in solitude, from going beyond the mere impression or symbol of growth and permanence. These unusual trees had seemed to make frantic gestures to him, almost as friends would have done in one last effort to render a deeper message.

Even though the narrator was unable to probe satisfactorily this phenomenon of the tree encounter, he did seem to derive from it a feeling of vibrant joy and inspiration. As he rode along, the birds flitting from tree to tree seemed to prolong the charm of the experience;[9] and his subsequent remarks upon the road upon which he was travelling were admirable:

[7]   This number, three, occurs in the case of the steeples of Martinville, of three farmhouses just out of Combray (I, 182) seen as Marcel was returning from one of his *randonnées* and in the *rencontre* of three persons, St.-Loup, Rachel, Marcel (II, 160) before fruit trees.

[8]   It is interesting to note the presence of a second person in a carriage. Such a presence often affected encounters in the recurrent carriage situation. (Reference is here made, e.g., to the presence of a second person on the carriage seat in Marcel's *clochers de Martinville* experience. The uncommunicative coachman, in this case, however, rendered the encounter fecund, for he did not interrupt Marcel's trend of thought; but when Albertine was with Marcel (III, 27 & 561), she *prevented* encounters; and, in fact, he felt there was always some "grave personne" present to prevent the most desirable encounters). This problem of persons as obstacles to encounters is seen in connection with Marcel's ever being on the search of a *rencontre tellement souhaitée* of a girl.

[9] This experience and its description seemed to be so meaningful that it appears in *Sodome et Gomorrhe*, thinly disguised under other circumstances, and almost verbatim (II, 994).

Raccordées à celles [he is referring to impressions] que j'éprouvais maintenant dans un autre pays, sur une route semblable, s'entourant de toutes les sensations accessoires de libre respiration, de curiosité, d'indolence, d'appétit, de gaieté qui leur étaient communes, exculant toutes les autres, ces impressions se renforceraient, prendraient la consistance d'un type particulier de plaisir, et presque d'un cadre d'existence que j'avais d'ailleurs rarement l'occasion de retrouver, mais dans lequel le réveil des souvenirs mettait au milieu de la réalité évoquée, songée, insaisissable, pour me donner, au milieu de ces régions où je passais, plus qu'un sentiment esthétique, un désir fugitif mais exalté, d'y vivre désormais pour toujours.[10]

If he is not hinting at the artistic vocation revealed by such encounters, he is at least entertaining the idea of the "bonheur même d'exister"[11] and "la réalité merveilleuse de cette vie, sa vie, unique, irremplaçable".[12]

When St.-Loup took Marcel along to meet Rachel, the former's mistress, the rencontre with fruit-trees at a Parisian suburb illustrates clearly the symbolistic significance to be found in Proust's plants. Cherry-trees in blossom, lilacs waving in the breeze, and pear-trees in a quincunx, or once in a group of three (II, 155), are the background for the above-mentioned rendez-vous. These plants, described alternately as fine cloths and hovering angels, witness Marcel's meeting with Rachel, in what he recognized as a disturbing re-encounter with a prostitute. Furthermore, the flowering fruit-trees are a setting for St.-Loup's innocent and enthusiastic expressions of love for Rachel. Transitory blossoms are met when love – that so unstable element with Proust – is at play. They symbolize CHANGE, "cette grande idée de Proust: notre vie...est en évolution perpétuelle".[13] Treated as "gardiens des souvenirs de l'âge d'or" and "garants que la réalité n'est pas ce qu'on croit" (I, 160), such plants symbolize not only change, but again, a certain degree of temporal permanence, along with inno- cence, unreality, and final reality. Marcel had looked in upon the

[10]   I, 721.
[11]   Germaine Brée, *Du Temps perdu au temps retrouvé*, p. 33.
[12]   *Ibid*, p. 10.
[13]   Léon Pierre-Quint; *Marcel Proust, sa vie, son oeuvre*, p. 14.

St-Loup–Rachel relationship as plants met with underlined its 'shaky' nature.

A similar rencontre (II, 781) with evanescent blossoms occurred at a time when his love-affair with Albertine was beginning. We refer to a scene symbolic of both transition and dominated Time. Marcel, on a warm, spring day, had discovered pink apple blossoms that remained ever aloft as, later in the day, a chilling rain beat down upon them. The persistent beauty of these flowers, destined, anyway, to fall soon, and the strong, upright branches bearing them seemed, too, to have special meaning for the narrator at a time when he had been brooding over his grandmother's death.

What is especially common to these two rencontres is that they serve to join humans and things. Other comparable examples are the association of Mademoiselle (later Madame) Stermaria with the poplars of the Bois de Boulogne (II, 384) or of Albertine with trees in the same Bois (III, 175). Furthermore, Marcel sometimes saw plants through people: people who recalled for him hawthorns, (I, 185)–or people changed into plants, as is the case, for example, of Gilberte presented as a lilac bush (I, 564).

We return, in one last analysis of a textual passage, to the idea of mystical beckoning in plants. We refer to a passage in *La Recherche* of paramount importance to this whole thesis of the Appel. It is not in itself an encounter, but, rather, an enunciation of principles that shall be born out throughout the novel:

Je trouve très raisonnable la croyance celtique que les âmes de ceux que nous avons perdus sont captives dans quelque être inférieur, dans une bête, un *végétal*, une *chose inanimée*,[14] perdues en effet pour nous jusqu'au jour, qui, pour beaucoup ne vient jamais, où nous nous trouvons passer près de l'arbre, entrer en possession de l'objet qui est leur prison. Alors elles *tressaillent*, nous appellent, et sitôt que nous les avons reconnues, l'enchantement est brisé. Délivrées par nous, elles ont vaincu la mort et reviennent vivre avec nous. Il en est ainsi de notre passé. C'est peine perdue que nous cherchons à l'évoquer, tous les efforts de notre intelligence sont inutiles. Il est caché hors de son domaine et de sa portée, en quelque objet materiel (en la sensation que nous donnerait

---

[14] The italicizing is my own.

cet objet matériel) que nous ne soupçonnons pas. Cet objet, il dépend du hasard que nous le rencontrions avant de mourir, ou que nous ne le rencontrions pas.[15]

Indeed, for many throughout the ages, the tree has possessed supernatural forces: Druids and certain Hindu priests actually believed in souls imprisoned in some *végétal*. In literature, the tree Tancred cut ran blood (13th Canto of *La Gerusalema liberata*). Proust's protagonist, in contemplating plants, presumably had near super-sensory powers to combine with his keen intelligence in order to grasp plants' messages – supernatural or not.

The passage quoted occurs in "Combray", immediately after the "drame du coucher", when Marcel's mother read *François le Champi* to calm the nervous child. Even more significantly, the passage comes immediately before the *madeleine* incident, which was to resurrect Combray by way of involuntary memory.

The quotation illustrates the principal problem of this study (how the *chance* encounter with inanimate objects stimulates *involuntary* memory). It introduces clearly Proust's idea of the inefficacy of *voluntary* memory. It brings into play, in its concluding sentences, the idea of the actual need for rencontre if (the) involuntary memory is to be stimulated. All this (written in a style exuding a certain *mysticité* remindful of the Symbolists) depends upon *chance*. In the first half of the quotation much stress is laid upon *plants* as mediums of such rencontres.

This special appeal of a tree is true because a plant, perhaps, in this panorama of chance meetings with natural objects, calls forth a response, more than other forces[16] and things, from all five senses: in the *smell* of blossoms, bark, pollen, and crushed leaves; in the *touch* of flowers and nodules; in the *sound* of rustling leaves; in distinctive *tastes*, for example, of camphor or sweet-bay leaves; in the myriad *shades* of green or in the florescence of spring blossoming. This last appeal is, of course, to *visual* perception –

---

[15]   I, 44.

[16]   By 'forces' we mean natural forces, like the phenomena of weather, the vibrational energy, or 'force', known as sound, etc.

perhaps the keenest of sensory capacities and resultant sensations of both Proust and his Narrator. As we have indicated, the latter was conscious early of the shape and shade of the apple-tree leaf, of the quaking and shimmering of a poplar leaf, and of the linear perspective and upright position of trees.

Finally, let us consider the rencontres with plants as mooring-points in the novel. There is clear, sharp symmetry in the meaning-ful appearance of the lilacs, apple-trees, and hawthorns early in "Combray" and the reappearance of trees (though a discouraging one) in *Le Temps retrouvé*, as Marcel's train came to an abrupt stop in the countryside (III, 885).

To summarize, we have shown, along general lines, that the rencontres in this category have symbolistic significance, illustrate balance and symmetry, and link natural objects with human beings. More specifically, we have demonstrated that these ren-contres are symbols of chance and change: occasionally they represent spiritual growth and dominated Time in this chaotic yet ordered world; they have strong appeal because they can evoke all five of the senses; they serve, just as do churches and rooms, as 'pile foundations' or as landmarks along the novel's route; they are linked with persons or characters of the novel as: (a) in a form of transmutation, (b) an object of association, and (c) a setting for rencontres of persons. This last-mentioned phenomenon and literary device is in itself a double-rencontre.

UNSEASONABLE WEATHER

(Analysis of individual rencontres and synthesis of their general significance)

Unseasonable weather and unexpectedly appearing fog or sunlight have in Proust's novel a pattern and a purpose. False spring, pre(-mature) spring, as early as the latter part of January or the beginning of February, has a 'mystical' appeal. This meteorological phenomenon of spring in winter, the name of which is best rendered by the German *Vorfrühling*, is sufficiently impelling to impress

Change upon us. For Proust's narrator the summoning forth of meaningful experiences and ideas often demands a break in routine, a change from Habit.

On one of those days in a period when "l'hiver recevait jusqu'au soir la visite inopinée et radieuse d'une journée de printemps" (I, 405), the narrator had arrived at the peak of expectations in his budding love-affair with Gilberte. In such a meteorological and psychological atmosphere, he lay in wait "aux Champs-Elysées", ever anticipating his *rencontre souhaitée* that day. Given over to reverie, Marcel mused over the mysterious, unknown elements of the young girl's life. He attached particular importance to her parents – in one of his cerebral wanderings along the high-road of ASSOCIATION. In Marcel's case much of this dreaming had been stimulated by the brusque turn of the weather.

To complete the diptych of changing weather as both a rencontre and a setting for the Gilbertian experience, there is just the reverse situation later in *A l'Ombre des jeunes filles en fleurs* (I, 634):

A reappearing and persistent cold had seated itself in April, in "semaines glaciales mais déjà fleurissantes". This reverse situation of unseasonable weather proved that "l'hiver, le printemps, l'été, ne sont pas séparés par des cloisons aussi hermétiques que tend à le croire le boulevardier". It served to awaken Marcel's dormant *moi* and memories of Combray, including the steep little road of Tansonville. It is the setting for marked progress towards indifference for Gilberte and eventual oblivion. With a poetic touch the author added to that part of this scene taking place in Madame Swann's living room flowers known as *boules de neige*. They epitomized the two seasons in one.

Thus, Proust's antithetical situations (I, 405, and I, 634) could be expressed in a mathematical relationship to show once more with what balance and symmetry he constructed *La Recherche:*

spring in winter : growing love :: winter in spring :
disintegrating love for Gilberte

Such equilibrium is continued in the presentation of two rencontres which are opposites; yet they produce the same memory-evoking result. The first (II, 345) was a rencontre with suddenly occurring fog. The second (III, 11) was an encounter with suddenly appearing sunlight. From page 345 of *Le Côté de Guermantes*, at a point where Marcel had returned to Paris from Doncières (and just after his grandmother's death), there follows a passage from the first-mentioned of these rencontres:

Bien que ce fût simplement un dimanche d'automne, je venais de renaître, l'existence était intacte devant moi, car dans la matinée, après une série de jours doux, il avait fait un brouillard froid qui ne s'était levé que vers midi: or, un changement de temps suffit à recréer le monde et nous-mêmes. Jadis, quand le vent soufflait dans ma cheminée, j'écoutais les coups qu'il frappait contre la trappe avec autant d'émotion que si, pareils aux fameux coups d'archet par lesquels débute *la Symphonie en ut mineur,* ils avaient été les appels irrésistibles d'un mystérieux destin. Tout changement à vue de la nature nous offre une transformation semblable, en adaptant au mode nouveau des choses nos désirs harmonisés. La brume, dès le réveil, avait fait de moi, au lieu de l'être centrifuge qu'on est par les beaux jours, un homme replié, désireux du coin du lit partagé, Adam frileux en quête d'une Eve sédentaire, dans ce monde différent.

Memories of Doncières suddenly came to life for "le monde nouveau dans lequel le brouillard de ce matin m'avait plongé était un monde déjà connu de moi". This weather encounter was, too, an excellent, natural prelude to the *rencontre prolongée* with a furnace's sound – to be analyzed in the next chapter division.

The opposite rencontre on page 11, Volume III, showed how abruptly appearing sunlight could break the almost stultifying power of Habit:

Le soleil tout à coup jaunissait cette mousseline de verre, la dorait, et, découvrant doucement en moi un jeune homme plus ancien qu'avait caché longtemps l'habitude, me grisait de souvenirs, comme si j'eusse été en pleine nature devant des feuillages dorés où ne manquait même pas la présence d'un oiseau.

Such a rencontre in the introduction of *La Prisonnière* is especially remindful of Proust's real life. We know how he was usually forced to appreciate nature vicariously, because of his long periods of confinement: He had to look at flowers through window-panes or the glass of automobiles. Unable to go to the countryside itself, he captured all of it through a mere ray of light through a window. Of greater importance was the memory-evoking power of the sunlight and its symbolical import: Change through Chance; Memory through Change.

After weeks of bad weather, brightness could inspire the Narrator to sing a light musical air, for "Tant l'atmosphère, selon le hasard des jours, agit profondément sur notre organisme et tire des réserves obscures où nous les avions oubliées les mélodies inscrites que n'a pas déchiffrées notre mémoire." (II, 143).

Fog in Paris (II, 397), as Marcel was descending his stairway to join St.-Loup for an evening together, could revive Combray. More important was its serving as an *appel:*

> Entre cette année, d'ailleurs incertaine, de Combray et les soirs à Rivebelle revus tout à l'heure au-dessus des rideaux, quelles différences ! J'éprouvais à les percevoir un enthousiasme qui aurait pu être fécond si j'étais resté seul, et m'aurait évité ainsi le détour de bien des années inutiles par lesquelles j'allais encore passer avant que se déclarât *la vocation invisible dont cet ouvrage est l'histoire.*[17]

Hundreds of pages ahead of the moving message of the artistic vocation in *Le Temps retrouvé,* such an anticipatory note is stimulating.

To summarize, we have shown how rencontres with unseasonable or changing weather, besides heralding the general significance of chance encounters with the inanimate in the discovery of the artistic vocation mentioned above, have served to illustrate the three announced capital functions which are the core of this study:

1) *Symbolistic significance:* (a) This is, of course, most evident in the case of Change, which prods those "bogged down" in Habit. Some people come alive with new ideas at the approach of winter or again in spring. Others may constantly be full of ideas regardless of the time or season and disregard, even disdainfully, weather or seasons; but their ideas are not necessarily as penetrating, their

---

[17] The italicizing is my own.

reminiscences are not as stirring, nor is the expression of both as poetic as in the case of Marcel Proust. His "fits and starts" need not be disparaged when we witness the majestic literary production to which they gave rise: (b) Chance and a world of perpetual movement are equally apparent in changing weather; (c) it is no mere coincidence that embryonic and decaying love were announced by unseasonable spring and winter, respectively.

(2) *Balance and symmetry:* Item (c) above, along with alternating, complementary passages on spring or winter, and on unanticipated fog or sunlight, have illustrated adequately this Proustian trait. Encounters again have seemed to serve as mooring-points for an episode – the love-affair with Gilberte.

(3) *Linking persons:* In some of the rencontres quoted, Gilberte, Mme Swann, and Albertine have been associated with the setting. Again, almost as much as with trees, *La Recherche* has, through things and forces themselves, joined the two spheres, human and inanimate.

SOUNDS AND ODORS

One of the interesting aspects of Proust's rencontres with sounds and odors is their pattern. First, in a type of recurring contrast, a recurrent pattern is seen vividly among many sound-odor rencontres we listed.[18] Let us note the inclusion of: both the homely and the more artistically appealing or even elegant objects, the crude and the refined, the coarse and the delicate. Proust pits the harsh sounds of a central heating system and a water-pipe's vibrations against the music of Vinteuil or a happily-timed gust of wind: He 'runs the gamut' of odors, from those of automobile oil or of a dank, public *pavillon* to those of Madame Swann's perfume or the rich and delicate household wares of Combray. Some of the latter odors, as those of preserved fruit or baked bread, are described as follows:

C'étaient de ces chambres de province qui–de même qu'en certains pays des parties entières de l'air ou de la mer sont illuminées ou parfumées par des myriades de protozoaires que nous ne voyons pas–nous enchantent des mille odeurs qu'y dégagent les vertus, la sagesse, les

18 Pages 24–26 of this study.

habitudes, toute une vie secrète, invisible, surabondante et morale que l'atmosphère y tient en suspens; odeurs naturelles encore, certes, et couleur du temps comme celles de la campagne voisine, mais déjà casanières, humaines et renfermées, gelée exquise, industrieuse et limpide de tous les fruits de l'année qui ont quitté le verger pour l'armoire:...[19]

Contrast of a different nature is seen, too, in the Narrator's reaction to Vinteuil's music as compared with and opposed to Swann's reaction. We have shown[20] how the latter was less successful than the Narrator in responding to the deepest message and full import of the *petite phrase.*

In addition to illustrating symmetry and equilibrium (in the passages just cited), a tendency to associate people and forces of nature, and a certain symbolism (as in the case of the *petite phrase* as a materialization of Swann's love), this series of rencontres inspires two other concluding thoughts:

First, the reactions of Proust and his Marcel to sounds and smells are those of a hypersensitive organism. On the negative side, he had to avoid his beloved flowers and plants because of his asthmatic condition; and he had objections to noise as strong as any of Montaigne or of Schopenhauer. The latter's vituperations against the cracking of whips in the street are no more expressive than the action of having a room sound-proofed with cork. On the other hand, Proust and the Narrator were both possessed of a soulful appreciation not merely of beauty but of the associative value of humble things within their intimate lives. In his search for truth, total truth, Proust pits the near-ridiculous against the sublime and the even possibly disagreeable against the agreable.

Secondly, with the exception of the madeleine experience, where *odor* was almost as vital as *taste*, none of the olfactory sensations evoked involuntary memory or the artistic vocation as forcibly as was the case with the aural sensations. The moldy, musty odor

---

[19]   I, 49.
[20]   In Chapter I, p. 17, of H. Kopman: *The Phenomenon of Rencontre in Proust's "A la Recherche du Temps Perdu".*

(I, 492) had not nearly the decisive compulsive force of the "cuiller contre une assiette" or "le bruit strident d'une conduite d'eau" (III, 868 and 874).

NAMES

As is true elsewhere in literature and life, names of people and places in *La Recherche* prove symbolically fecund; but in *La Recherche* we feel that the very syllables of certain names are musical notes, notes that even take on colors.

In Proust's work, the name is often the springboard for that game of imagination versus reality that so preoccupied him. The reality of the rencontre with persons or places that had once been glorified in the imagination through the form of a magical name is temporarily paralyzing. Marcel had come upon the name of Guermantes many times; but his first rencontre with Mme de Guermantes at the marriage of Mlle Percepied is naturally more fascinating. We see here a temporary paralysis by reality and subsequently a fusing of reality and the original imagination. We consider the imagined duchess of the *rencontre souhaitée*, we are then impressed by the first actual meeting with the lady "au grand nez", and finally we see Marcel's fusion of the lady present and the imagined duchess. While "the external world perceived by his five senses will never resemble the harmonious inner world created by his imagination"[21] (that inner world created earlier through rencontres with the NAME), Marcel, here, in this church scene, eventually rendered an image ever more powerful by blending the present reality and his first imaginings.

Of all the names met, this one of Guermantes is the most important. It represents persons and a place–a way of life and a way of walking along a river bank, an aesthetic preoccupation with French and Germanic heraldry, an *esprit*, and, finally, a woman, first to be admired, then to be discredited. Throughout the *Recherche* there have been present what may be termed the "Guermantes

[21] F. M. Green, *The Mind of Proust*, p. 61.

Rencontres"–with the people, his imaginary rencontres with the
country estate,[22] and very name.

In the various name-rencontres we have singled out[23] in this
chapter, the names of Gilberte and Madame de Guermantes occur
most frequently. They and their names are often associated with
a puff of wind, a gust of air, or a general atmosphere of mystical
rapture. For example, Marcel, in a stroll Swann's-Way, had heard
Gilberte's name called out, "donné comme un talisman qui me
permettrait peut-être de retrouver un jour celle dont il venait
de faire une personne et qui, l'instant d'avant n'était qu'une image
incertaine" (I, 141–2). Later, in *A l'Ombre des jeunes filles en
fleurs* (I, 394), Marcel heard the same while at play on a lawn just
off the Champs-Elysées:

> Ce nom de Gilberte passa près de moi, évoquant d'autant plus
> l'existence de celle qu'il désignait qu'il ne la nommait pas seulement
> comme un absent dont on parle, mais l'interpellait; il passa ainsi près
> de moi, en action pour ainsi dire, avec une puissance qu'accroissait la
> courbe de son jet et l'approche de son but;...

Finally, it is of interest to note that such names, particularly
Guermantes, are linked not only to love, the social world and
inconsequential dreaming but also to the Narrator's respect for
the virtues of Combray and his goal of becoming a writer, to his
feeling for perfection:

> Ainsi, au hasard de cette rencontre d'idées, d'images, et de sentiment,
> naît un monde accroché à des êtres; à des lieux réels, qui bénéficie de
> son association avec les idées puisées à Combray, en particulier l'idée
> de perfection et de beauté.[24]

and:

> Il suffit qu'un nom ou qu'une image appartenant à ce monde vienne
> le frôler, pour qu'immédiatement la vie prenne pour lui une intense
> réalité.[25]

---

[22]   Marcel never actually encountered the estate; hence the power of the
Name.

[23]   Chapter II. p. 107 of: H. Kopman: *The Phenomenon of Rencontre in
Proust's A la Recherche du Temps perdu.*

[24]   Brée, *op. cit.*, p. 37.

[25]   *Ibid.*, p. 38.

In analyzing the rôle of the name, we are already moving towards the conclusion of the novel. The force of the name was so great that, for example, the patronymic, Guermantes, heard in later years "breathed the air of Combray of that particular year" and served to set into motion the chain-reaction of rencontres[26] of *Le Temps retrouvé*, which we shall review presently.

Names, like other sounds, forces, natural elements, and inanimate objects, have shown in encounters in *La Recherche* that they furthered balance, served as symbols and were associated with people (as "Ce nom devenu pour moi presque mythologique de Swann" and its connection with Gilberte – or "Touraine" associated with Albertine).

We have shown, too, that names are an excellent medium for Proust's theme of imagination-reality. We note, too, that one name alone, Guermantes, could support a whole series of encounters in its own isolated category.

Finally, we are becoming increasingly conscious of a web of rencontre, a filigrane pattern corresponding to that of the rencontres of people with other people throughout the novel. Trees, leaves, music, gusts of wind, NAMES, places, people, sound, light, and odors are relayed by one another; and they are related to one another. We find intermingling and intertwining throughout.

PLACES

(embracing not only cities and towns but also buildings, churches, streets and country estates)

Besides Venice and Balbec,[27] we have included churches, the Tansonville property, a park, and even a street in the category, "places".

The first rencontre in *La Recherche* within this category of places

[26] Called "explosions" by Clive Bell in his essay, *Marcel Proust* (London, 1928).
[27] As noted in Chapter II, pages 208–209 of: H. Kopman: *The Phenomenon of Rencontre in Proust's A la Recherche du Temps perdu.*

will be with a church. Very few pages beyond the beginning of the long and unforgettable description of Combray, one reads:

Que je l'aimais, que je la revois bien, notre Eglise ! Son vieux porche par lequel nous entrions, noir, grêle comme une écumoire, était dévié et profondément creusé aux angles (de même que le bénitier où il nous conduisait) comme si le doux effleurement des mantes des paysannes entrant à l'église et de leurs doigts timides prenant de l'eau bénite, pouvait, répété pendant des siècles, acquérir une force destructive, infléchir la pierre et l'entailler de sillons comme en trace la roue des carrioles dans la borne contre laquelle elle bute tous les jours.[28]

There follows a detailed description embracing no fewer than eight pages. This description may not be a 'rencontre-reminiscence', but it does prepare the reader for many re-encounters throughout *La Recherche*.

One moves along through highly-coloured passages describing, after consideration of the church's tombs, stained-glass windows and highwarp tapestry. Then the Narrator declares that:

Tout cela, et plus encore, les objets précieux venus à l'église de personnages qui étaient pour moi presque des personnages de légende... tout cela faisait d'elle pour moi quelque chose d'entièrement différent du reste de la ville: un édifice occupant, si l'on peut dire, un espace à quatre dimensions—la quatrième étant celle du Temps—déployant à travers les siècles son vaisseau, qui de travée en travée, de chapelle en chapelle, semblait vaincre et franchir, non pas seulement quelques mètres mais des époques successives, d'où il sortait victorieux...[29]

After this passage on the church's victory over Time, a description of the unpretentious apse or *abside* of the little church shows that Proust and his narrator were often drawn by the simplest and humblest of things. Next comes a series of passages indicating the significance of the steeple:

Et dans une des plus grandes promenades que nous faisions de Combray, il y avait un endroit où la route resserrée débouchait tout à coup sur un immense plateau fermé à l'horizon par des forêts déchiquetées que dépassait seule la fine pointe du clocher de Saint-Hilaire, mais si mince, si rose, qu'elle semblait seulement rayée sur le ciel par

[28]   I, p. 59.
[29]   I, p. 61.

un ongle qui aurait voulu donner à ce paysage, à ce tableau rien que
de nature, cette petite marque d'art, cette unique indication humaine...;
et, par un matin brumeux d'automne, on aurait dit, s'élevant au-dessus
du violet orageux des vignobles, une ruine de pourpre presque de la
couleur de la vigne vierge.[30]

In the style of a verbal landscape artist, this and following descriptions of the steeple out of which the *corbeaux*[31] flew show how the
church-tower overlooked and dominated all Combray.

The Narrator maintained that this church was "une partie
profonde de ma vie". Again, it is something that epitomizes
familiar, intimate things in one's own life. It points toward one
of the chief themes of the novel: remembrance of things attached
to one's own existence. It announces already what Proust and
his narrator, later in the novel, and especially in *Le Temps retrouvé*,
will acknowledge as the only truth, the only reality: recognition
of the value of such intimate reminiscences.

"L'Eglise! familière; mitoyenne, rue Saint-Hilaire..." It was
a simple, unpretentious church, what with its crudely constructed
apse. But it was *his* church, landmark of *his* Combray. Such
veneration illustrates another of Proust's chief aesthetic themes
mentioned repeatedly in this chapter: choosing "les choses les
plus humbles" (a simple landscape, an unpretentious church apse)
and 're-creating' them.

Other church steeples caught the Narrator's eye; and asking
them to render their message, he would end in saying, "je cherche
encore mon chemin, je tourne une rue...mais...c'est dans mon
coeur". (I, 67). What he meant was that his true reality was linked
with reminiscences of the simple little church of Combray, in
remembrance of things past, intimate, and deep-seated.

This rencontre illustrating the dominant rôle of the church in
Proust's novel, with its dazzling color and provocative historical
reference to Dagobert, was meaningful because the church was:
(a) time-defying; (b) beautiful and bright inside even in bad weather
because of the stained glass windows; (c) the only human fabrication,

---

[30]   I, p. 63.
[31]   More likely *choucas* or *corneilles d'église*.

and one that could harmonize with nature, in a natural scene of the tree-tops of Combray; (d) possessed of a belfry that evoked the same visual response as would the towers of Martinville; (e) associated with the forebears of the Guermantes; (f) the place where Marcel first encountered Madame de Guermantes; (g) symbolical of two themes: (1) "les choses les plus humbles", and (2) greater reality and truth to be uncovered in one's intimate experiences; (h) finally, both a mooring-point and a launching base, an example of architectural-literary balance, pointed out ever so often by André Maurois and other critics of Proust.

More Proustian symmetry is seen in the next two rencontres with natural objects and the natural scene. The attentive reader must surely be aware of their balance and contrast: The closing of the chapter, "Noms de Pays: le Pays", at the end of *A l'Ombre des jeunes filles en fleurs*, calls to mind the ending of the chapter, "Noms de Pays: le Nom". Proust terminates this latter-mentioned part of the book dealing with a certain phase of his narrator's Gilbertian affair (which was to last almost two years) with a grey sky, a rippling Grand Lac of the Bois de Boulogne, migrating birds and leafless trees. When we read the ending of *A l'Ombre des jeunes filles en fleurs*, stamped with more bleak weather and the abandonment of Balbec by tourists, we think back upon the close of "Noms de Pays: Le Nom".

Rencontres with places, besides having such import as observed in the case of Saint-Hilaire Church and the just-mentioned example of equilibrium, are of consequence in that they are connected with people, characters of the novel – be it the Bois de Boulogne as a place for possibly meeting Madame de Stermaria or a search for a street in Venice that reminds us of the *rencontre rêvée* and *recherchée* of a woman.[32] Besides illustrating the theme of alternating

---

[32]   Indeed a fitting prelude to the almost droll search for the maid of the Baronne de Putbus. Here, Proust's human comedy of such misdirected *recherche*, disillusionment and oblivion in love, disappointment in his friend Saint-Loup and general deception with the world of people, is now ripe for the "thème du découragement", something to be introduced in two significant encounters in the last division of the novel, *Le Temps retrouvé*.

encouragement and discouragement (Tansonville in "Combray"–
Tansonville in the first pages of *Le Temps retrouvé*), rencontres
with places underline the conflict of imagination and reality. The
place imagined, dreamed of, glorified through its very magical
name, can (as the Balbec church) prove to be a place hardly
inspiring upon actual confrontation.

RENCONTRES WITH OBJECTS INTIMATELY RELATED WITH THE NOVEL'S CHARACTERS

A common device in literature is the association of some object
with a novel's character. This situation, more often than not,
comes within an episode of love. Proust, so conscious of this form
of reminiscence through inanimate objects, has given us numerous
examples of such a phenomenon. In the tabular listing under this
particular category, Albertine's rings discovered after her depar-
ture (III, 462) furnish a typical example. The narrator was reminded
later of his 'fugitive' by a bench or a moonbeam (III, 481). As for
rooms,[33] Proust assigned to them, in examples too numerous to
comment, a vital importance as a place of meeting, a locale of
experience. The associative value of Vinteuil's music, equally
important, pervades the work.

In what we are beginning to recognize more and more as a
veritable filagree of rencontre, the *petite phrase* has linked its
composer, his daughter, Albertine, Léa, Morel, and Marcel by the
time we have read through *La Fugitive*. This is a marked development (of the piece of music and its significance) from its modest
beginning as a symbol of Swann's one-time, compelling love for
Odette (I, 345).

Because of its evocation of that Proustian phenomenon known
as the *intermittences du coeur*, we have chosen for analysis Marcel's
rencontre with a shoe-button and his awareness of a gesture involved
in reaching for it. More than a year after the death of his grandmother, whom he had not always appreciated as fully as he might,

[33]   E.g., III, 542 (Albertine's room in Paris).

Marcel made a second visit to Balbec. Once, in his hotel room, by the sudden bending movement he made to lace his shoes, he recalled the kindness his grandmother had once displayed in helping him, the semi-invalid, with his painful dressing.

He felt a moment of penetrating revelation just as expressive as the experiences with the madeleine and the steeples of Martinville. In *Sodome et Gomorrhre* (page 756) Marcel saw vividly his grandmother's face in all its tenderness–for the first time since her death:

J'avais souvent parlé d'elle depuis ce moment-là et aussi pensé à elle, mais sous mes paroles et mes pensées de jeune homme ingrat, égoïste et cruel, il n'y avait jamais rien eu qui ressemblât à ma grand' mère, parce que dans ma légèreté, mon amour du plaisir, mon accoutumance à la voir malade, je ne contenais en moi qu'à l'état virtuel le souvenir de ce qu'elle avait été. A n'importe quel moment que nous la considérons, notre âme totale n'a qu'une valeur presque flctive, malgré le nombreux bilan de ses richesses, car tantôt les unes, tantôt les autres sont indisponibles, qu'il s'agisse d'ailleurs de richesses effectives aussi bien que de celles de l'imagination, et pour moi par exemple, tout autant que de l'ancien nom de Guermantes, de celles, combien plus graves, du souvenir vrai de ma grand'mère. Car aux troubles de la mémoire sont liées les intermittences du coeur. C'est sans doute l'existence de notre corps, semblable pour nous à un vase où notre spiritualité serait enclose, qui nous enduit à supposer que tous nos biens intérieurs, nos joies passées, toutes nos douleurs sont perpétuellement en notre possession.

He had experienced an actual *deuxième rencontre* with her. This phenomenon, as well as his full realization of her death, pivoted upon a chance sensation. Only a fortuitous movement could release his *moi*. An earlier *moi*, yet one independent of time, had in it a core of genuine affection.

The Narrator thought that:

Cette impression si douloureuse et actuellement incompréhensible, je savais, non certes pas si j'en dégagerais un peu de vérité un jour, mais que si, ce peu de vérité, je pouvais jamais l'extraire, ce ne pourrait être que d'elle, si particulière, si spontanée, qui n'avait été ni tracée par mon intelligence, ni atténuée par ma pusillanimité, mais que la mort elle-même, la brusque révélation de la mort, avait, comme la foudre, creusée en moi, selon un graphique surnaturel, inhumain, comme un double et mystérieux sillon.[34]

Thus, a rencontre with an inanimate object has served as a discovery, a revelation. It has brought back his grandmother, it has impressed her death upon him, and it has made him aware of the process known as the "intermittences du coeur".

Natural objects have served frequently to revive memories of people. Many in *La Recherche* have served as symbols. What is more, a number of the meetings with natural objects or forces (as the case of Swann, the *petite phrase*, his love for Odette, I, 345) reveal a common and important element – an evocation of the *intermittences du coeur* just described. We might term such encounter-revelations as "un peu d'affection à l'état pur"–not too far removed from "un peu de temps à l'état pur", which we are about to examine in *Le Temps retrouvé*.

Well before enouncing it in *Le Temps retrouvé*, Proust is supporting his thesis that intelligence and voluntary memory cannot reproduce the past as do these fortuitous experiences such as the meeting with the shoe-button – an encounter that has roused his heart.

RENCONTRE WITHIN *LE TEMPS RETROUVÉ*

In its established text, this last division of the novel opens with an uninspired Marcel viewing what he once held as the incantations of Combray. Tansonville is no longer appealing; and those challenging mysteries of yesteryear, making for the charm of childhood, such as the alluringly remote source of the Vivonne or the Guermantes' estate, now mean very little. Only one common link with boyhood days now remains, and it is a negative one: Marcel's feeling, as on these particular walks, that he will never be a writer. Even when the church tower is suddenly perceived (III, 698), he goes no further than to note its distance in time and space.

[34]   II, 759.

Later, Marcel returned to Paris from a "nouvelle maison de santé" (III, 854) by train. During this trip, the line of trees seen from the railway carriage is hardly a pure reminiscence but is surely a disheartening rencontre. It is Marcel's disillusionment with nature, that Nature, which Wordsworth said, was "the only friend not to betray us". Yet it had betrayed as had literature and the world of people. How could he even speak of the nearby flowers? He asked himself, "Peut-on espérer transmettre au lecteur un plaisir qu'on n'a pas ressenti?"

This is an experience with the *néant*, not unlike that of the existentialist before attaining his *Eigentlichkeit* or *authenticité*. In spite of this *néant*, Marcel will soon know self-realization. He will recognize his artistic vocation, that of writing.

His literary force may be a great one, exceeding perhaps Balzac's, certainly the Goncourts'. These writers, as we know, lay great stock in descriptions that were often mere pictorial reproductions. On the other hand, the Narrator (as is true of Proust) will not rely on observation and careful documentation alone. He will employ the metaphor, recreate impressions, and produce realism greater than the realists'. His reality will be largely within himself. The following critical passage shows how Proust's writing differs from the Flaubertian type of description:

But by recreating the beam of sunlight that spilled upon the floor, the scent of lilac in the air, or the musty smell of old books, he can convey a sense of vividness and depth that any amount of detailed description is powerless to evoke.[35]

How does he make such a discovery? In his *recherche*, knocking at "toutes les portes", he discovers one that finally opens. "On y heurte" by a *chance sensation*, by a series of encounters with inanimate objects.

Certain critics maintain that this knocking at the proper door, this eventual revelation of the artistic vocation starts with the sensation (previously identified[36]) of the *pavés inégaux*, ends with

[35]   Derrick Leon, *Introduction to Proust*, p. 306.
[36]   Chapter II, p. 97, in: H. Kopman, *The Phenomenon of the Rencontre in Proust's "A la Recherche du Temps perdu"*,

the water-pipe sound. The whole process, however, began with the reencounter of the name of Guermantes, and we consider that the perception of the volume of *François le Champi* is an extension of the same experience. In fact, we might go back farther than that, maintaining that the whole experience got its impetus from the train-window encounter. The disheartening view of the uninspiring line of trees seen from the train-window came at a time when the Narrator was confused as to what literature and reality were. His general discouragement and his lagging interest in literary pursuits made him available to the social world, ready to accept the invitation to this particular matinée.

Yet, in the invitation to the matinée, it was the actual name, Guermantes, with its lingering aesthetic appeal, which "reprit pour moi le charme et la signification que je lui trouvais à Combray" (III, 856). Added to this is the fortuitous circumstance of the Prince of Guermantes' change of address. This unexpected change in residence led to a ride over streets directed towards the Champs-Elysées, over streets of memory, in what was a seemingly mystical experience of smooth sailing over rough pavement:

> Elles étaient fort mal pavées à ce moment-là, mais dès le moment où j'y entrai, je n'en fus pas moins détaché de mes pensées par cette sensation d'une extrême douceur qu'on a quand, tout d'un coup, la voiture roule plus facilement, plus doucement, sans bruit, comme quand, les grilles d'un parc s'étant ouvertes, on glisse sur les allées couvertes d'un sable fin ou de feuilles mortes; matériellement, il n'en était rien, mais je sentis tout d'un coup la suppression des obstacles extérieurs parce qu'il n'y avait plus pour moi l'effort d'adaptation ou d'attention que nous faisons, même sans nous en rendre compte, devant les choses nouvelles...[37]

The Narrator recently had been going through a phase of utter disillusionment. He had taken on a view of "existence toute en longueur", that is to say, a view that could not include any bend, curve, a cold eye. He was no longer guided by youthful reveries. But the chance ride over familiar streets did now move a responsive

[37] III, 858.

chord of memory and feeling. This carriage ride had the imprint of enchantment and served as a fitting prelude to the novel's most important rencontre–with the *pavés inégaux*.

While the Narrator was standing in the courtyard before the Guermantes' residence, he was almost run over. Thanks to an alert "wattman" or tramdriver, he was warned in time. This brusque warning, however, caused him to stumble against two uneven paving stones. In what has been termed a *moment privilégié*[38] and a *moment identique*, the Narrator experienced an unusual joy. This time he penetrated the meaning of such a vivid sensation. His reaction had been so strong because he had once had a similar feeling thanks to the uneven stones of San Marco's Baptistery in Venice. He was now, in present time, undergoing the very same experience. Its intensity and vividness were relayed to him by an almost supernatural recapture of the blueness of Venice. This flash of blue of yesteryear came to him at that very moment in the Guermantes' courtyard.

Once evoked, the phenomenon of involuntary memory was to recur in an astounding series of rapidly succeeding rencontres. Upon entering the Guermantes' mansion and waiting in an ante-room for the proper pause in their musical matinée, Marcel suddenly heard the sound of a spoon against a plate. This aural sensation was so keen that it was accompanied by one of smoke- and woods-odor.[39] He had been reminded of a hammer striking against the

---

[38]   We point out a certain similarity between the early pages of *Le Côté de Guermantes* I and *Le Temps retrouvé* II. On page 777 of this sensation of steps is already treated volumes ahead of the *pavés inégaux* incident in *Le Temps retrouvé*. The name of Guermantes is treated on pages 11 and 12 of *Le Côté de Guermantes* and serves as a matching piece for the name of Guermantes in the early pages of *Le Temps retrouvé*. We observe, too, that both involuntary memory and *moments identiques*, appear in preparatory passages on pages 12 and 30, resp., II.

[39]   This "cadre forestier" and a reference to the "même rangée d'arbres" takes us back to the discouraging *rencontre* with the trees seen from the stopped train (III, 854). A *"future"* encounter can seemingly *revivify* a seemingly insignificant *impression*. This is to say, in almost Sartrian terms, that the past is always open to reappraisal.

wheel of a train stopped in a French forest. When he was given
a starched napkin, memories of Balbec were revived. He remembered the same sensation of stiffness of his napkin used the first
day he ever spent at the memorable seaside resort.

Conscious of this startling prolongation of this unique, 'mystical'
series of experiences, or what we might term, 'electrical coincidences'. Proust's protagonist decided to make a deeper analysis.
This time he had gone much further than in his experiences with
the hawthorns or the three trees Hudemesnil-Way. He had actually
associated the *pavés inégaux* of two distinct experiences, past and
present. The Narrator deducted further that he could not reproduce
the same phenomenon by employing his imagination. One cannot
'imagine' a thing once hoped for and now realized in one's presence.
Imagination in present time cannot give us the reality we seek.
Direct observation in present time is powerless and unproductive.
Intelligence and *voluntary memory* cannot truly capture the past.
Will does not dominate the future. The following passage, however,
shows how the past is recaptured:

Mais qu'un bruit, qu'une odeur, déjà entendu ou respirée jadis, le
soient de nouveau, à la fois dans le présent et dans le passé, réels, sans
être actuels, idéaux sans être abstraits, aussitôt l'essence permanente
et habituellement cachée des choses se trouve libérée, et notre vrai
moi, qui parfois depuis longtemps, semblait mort, mais ne l'était pas
entièrement, s'éveille, s'anime en recevant la céleste nourriture qui lui
est apportée. Une minute affranchie de l'ordre du temps a recréé en
nous, pour la sentir, l'homme affranchi de l'ordre du temps.[40]

In a word, the experience of an earlier *moi* had been regained by
fortuitous sensory experiences. A rencontre had produced an
essence more important than either the present or the past
individually; this extracted essence Proust has named, "Un peu
de temps à l'état pur" (III, 872).

If we were perhaps inclined to find childish or absurd the next
rencontre with the vibrating sound of a water-pipe that invites
the memory to reproduce the sound of boat whistles off Balbec
we would rejoice in the Huxlean condemnation of "Proust and

his miserable past". But cannot the rank odor of milk-weed, ragweed,[41] or some other crude yet pungent wild plant evoke a highland pasture, a place full of charm? This rencontre is to be taken most seriously and arouses all the senses of Proust's protagonist to a full and meaningful recapture of another lost paradise.

After this fourth and last of that particular series of rencontres coming in such rapid succession, the Narrator arrived at further conclusions. He realized now that these reminiscences were closely related to impressions that had, too, served as appeals. The experience of unequal paving stones, then, was intimately connected with the joy felt upon seeing the steeples of Martinville. In either case he found it necessary to "interpréter les sensations comme les signes d'autant de lois et d'idées, en essayant de penser, c'est-à-dire, de faire sortir de la pénombre ce que j'avais senti, de le convertir en un équivalent spirituel" (III, 879). An "équivalent spirituel" can best be rendered through the vocation of writing.

Of further importance is the Narrator's recognition of the rôle of chance in his recent rencontres:

Je n'avais pas été chercher les deux pavés inégaux de la cour où j'avais buté. Mais justement la façon fortuite, inévitable, dont la sensation avait été rencontrée, contrôlait la vérité du passé qu'elle ressuscitait, des images qu'elle déclenchait, puisque nous sentons son effort pour remonter vers la lumière, que nous sentons la joie du réel retrouvé.[42]

Some pages later, in an extension of the same general experience, the chance discovery in the Guermantes' library of the copy of *François le Champi* seems to complete an arch from name to name, from Guermantes to *François le Champi*, to connect pages 856 and 883. This final rencontre of the series recalls the most important evening perhaps in the narrator's early life. Instead of having an aura of azur, it is attuned to a little sadness; for we must not forget that while Proust's *rencontres* do invite a world of exhilaration,

[41] But an odor not recommended for a Proust with an unfortunate asthmatic condition.
[42] III, p. 879.

A la Recherche du Temps perdu has neither the serenity of assured spiritual achievement nor the unrelieved pessimism of the cynical materialist; what it does give is a somber panorama of time lit by flashes of eternity.[43]

In any case,

La vue de la couverture d'un livre déjà lu a tissé dans les caractères de son titre les rayons de lune d'une lointaine nuit d'été.[44]

More important is the fact that in analysing his rencontre with *François le Champi*, "un livre sous sa couverture rouge comme les autres", the Narrator realizes that his literary message will be not merely to 'describe things', to function as a so-called 'realist'. No, *François le Champi* has revived his former *moi* and emphasized for him his inner reality. Here, in his own words, is what the experience meant to him:

Mais c'est plus volontiers de l'histoire de ma propre vie, c'est-à-dire non pas en simple curieux, que je la[45] dégagerais; et ce serait souvent non pas à l'exemplaire matériel que je l'attacherais, mais à l'ouvrage, comme à ce *François le Champi*, contemplé pour la première fois dans ma petite chambre de Combray, pendant la nuit peut-être la plus douce et la plus triste de ma vie où j'avais, hélas (dans un temps où me paraissaient bien inaccessibles les mystérieux Guermantes) obtenu de mes parents une première abdication d'où je pouvais faire dater le déclin de ma santé et de mon vouloir, mon renoncement chaque jour aggravé à une tâche difficile—et retrouvé aujourd'hui dans la bibliothèque des Guermantes précisément, par le jour le plus beau et dont s'éclairaient soudain non seulement les tâtonnements anciens de ma pensée, mais même le but de ma vie et peut-être de l'art. (III, 887)

Furthermore, *François le Champi* may once have symbolized an abandonment of the will; but Marcel's new experience with the volume had stimulated the will to produce, the drive towards artistic production.

By this point in the novel, Marcel had a conception of the "greatness of art, true art" (III, 895). This greatness consists of

---

[43]   March, *op. cit.*, p. 250.
[44]   III, p. 889.
[45]   [la beauté]

"regaining or rediscovering what is quite simply one's own life" (III, 895).

Since much of the remainder of "La Matinée chez la Princesse de Guermantes" is devoted to either speculation or to the final meeting of the characters of the novel, there remain for comment only two more rencontres with the inanimate:

By chance an invitation card dropped from Marcel's workbook evoked the conflict between the worlds of artistry and social activity (III, 1040); and, finally, there is a reencounter different from all those commented upon thus far; the second encounter within the depth of the soul with the little bell of Combray,[46] a compelling bell, inducing Marcel to produce a work of art based upon a recaptured past:

Pour tâcher de l'entendre de plus près, c'est en moi-même que j'étais obligé de redescendre. C'est donc que ce tintement y était toujours, et aussi, entre lui et l'instant présent, tout ce passé indéfiniment déroulé que je ne savais pas que je portais.[47]

The Narrator had been on a long search for "greener pastures". He had been imbued with the Russian proverb, "The bells on the other side of the mountain tinkle more sweetly." Now, as he listened to the Combray bell, he felt that he was on both sides of that mountain. He had joined the past and the present. He had even belied the Roman dictum, *Mons non cum monte miscetur.* His rencontres had indeed caused inanimate and immovable objects and places, in different zones of time and space, to join one another. Most important of all, he had actually found a "greener pasture"– the literary calling. The Protagonist now had the inspiration and will to produce a work marked, as was the Combray church, with temporal permanence. He seemed ready to fight courageously against chronological Time in order to indite his experience with regained Time.

---

[46]   The small gate-bell at his aunt's Combray home, a bell that would often announce Swann's visits in "Combray".
[47]   III, p. 1046.

The chance encounter with the inanimate has truly given a steely structure to *Le Temps retrouvé*. Proust does not claim a monopoly on such experiences. He acknowledged their presence and seemingly mystical significance in the works of Chateaubriand and Baudelaire; but most significant to this investigation is Proust's statement that Baudelaire's experiences lacked the *fortuitous* character of his own. Baudelaire sought voluntarily. Proust's most meaningful *rencontres* with inanimate objects were *chance encounters*.

We have shown how rencontres earlier in the novel were constantly hinting at, leading up to, these ultimate, capital encounters in *Le Temps retrouvé*. These latter, especially the one with the *pavés inégaux*, proved to be such vivid phenomena because the Narrator was actually *reliving* these *experiences*. It is no wonder that they evoked for him his literary calling. However, all rencontres as reminiscences have proved vital:

A surprise, the taste of a madeleine soaked in tea, the phrase of a sonata by Vinteuil, the click of a lift as it passes a floor, the untying of a shoelace, the unbuttoning of an overcoat, such were the jolts that for him provoked explosion. *A La Recherche du temps perdu* is a series of carefully planned explosions by means of which the submerged past is brought into the present, the deep-sea monsters of memory to the surface. The pursuit, capture, and exhibition of these is the motive of the book.[48]

[48] Clive Bell, *Marcel Proust*, p. 41.

4

STRIKING IMPRESSIONS AND DESCRIPTIONS

While *impressions* are not *réminiscences* and may not always be chance encounters, they still are *rencontres* of first importance. Impressions form descriptive passages that serve as ideal complements to the reminiscences just treated and are complements, as well, to the world of human characters. Proust gave us well–documented pictures of the social life of his time. He made brilliant psychological analyses of his characters. He often wrote lively dialogues or interesting long speeches of the principal personages of the novel. He did not fail, however, to offer us variety by festooning his work with descriptive writing.

If one has tired of reading certain passages that describe the social world, there is relief and inspiring beauty to be found in the following lines that describe Marcel's first view of the sea at Balbec:

A tous moments, tenant à la main la serviette raide et empesée où était écrit le nom de l'Hôtel et avec laquelle je faisais d'inutiles efforts pour me sécher, je retournais près de la fenêtre jeter encore un regard sur ce vaste cirque éblouissant et montagneux et sur les *sommets neigeux de ses vagues en pierre d'émeraude* ça et là polie et translucide, lesquelles avec une placide violence et un froncement léonin laissaient s'accomplir et dévaler l'écroulement de leurs pentes auxquelles le soleil ajoutait un sourire sans visage... Et dès ce premier matin, le soleil me désignait au loin, d'un doigt souriant, *ces cimes bleues de la mer qui n'ont de nom sur aucune carte géographique....* (I, 672–3).

Proust's word-pictures that convey to us the magic of the restaurant at Rivebelle or of the Gare Saint-Lazare as seen through his eyes, that catch the play of light on Montjouvain pond, that make us appreciate the *puissance évocatrice* of fog, or that picture small mountains on the surface of the sea are plentiful.

We propose to list them in tabular form. This listing will be in the actual order of their appearance in *La Recherche*, volume by volume.

We propose next, following the above-mentioned order, to analyze briefly some of the more striking impressions-descriptions listed.

Here, then, before any discussion of the descriptive techniques of Proust, begins our tabular presentation:

VOLUME I

Page   51–description of dried *tilleul* leaves and stems

   59–67–architectural description of the Combray church

       72–at Combray a "coin de jardin" where one detected "un dallage rouge et luisant comme un porphyre"

       83–a metaphorical description in which light is rendered by sound: blows delivered in the street below the Combray house were practically metamorphosed for the narrator into the dazzling stars of bright summer light.

     112–the description of the hawthorns in the Combray church

     133–the red fish of dinner seen in the red glow of a sunset

     135–lilacs viewed during a promenade Swann's Way

     136–the fusion of natural growth and a man-made pond Swann's Way

     138–the first rencontre with the hawthorns in growth

     146–a first awareness of apple-trees

     150–a passage extending to page 152 and abounding in natural description: the rain, how summer weather hoists her violet or silken sails, the play of light along that fascinating border of the cloud and the sun's disk, a few random vignettes from "Combray" that illustrate writing real in its unreality

     156–the Gothic architecture of Saint-André-les-Champs

     162–an introduction to the charm of poplars

167–a tow-path which in summer was shaded by the "feuillage bleu d'un noisetier"

169–"le blanc et le rose proprets de la julienne, lavés comme de la porcelaine avec un soin domestique"–and passages beyond this, where one encounters the *boutons d'or* and the celebrated *nymphéas* of the Combray passage

179–les clochers de Martinville

383–one feels intensely the gusts of wind blowing along the Champs-Elysées and how they might be compared to those of a coastal area as Balbec

422–impressions of the Bois de Boulogne

596–the revelation of the metallic quality of the chrysanthemum flowers' colours and their correspondence to sunsets

672–the narrator's first view of the sea, at Balbec

704–the sea described as a "lieu de rencontre" (This has been listed under the heading of "reminiscences", too.)

715–a fascinating, shimmering "façade vegétale" of a Norman church

802–embracing several pages, here begins an example of the author's *re-création* that gives a double metaphor of church *retable* and precious jewel setting in a sea-sun scene of Balbec.

836–the famous seascape-landscape of Elstir, one that epitomized Proustian impressions

Volume II

12–Phrased in some of Proust's best writing, and exuding periwinkle blue, sinople, green, azure, mauve, orange, and violet in a color orgy, this beginning of *Le Côté de Guermantes I* seems something of a companion piece to the early part of *Le Temps retrouvé II*, what with the same reckoning with the force of the Name.

40–that unusual description of the *baignoire* of the Princesse de Guermantes at the *Opéra*.

83–the description of Marcel's room at Doncières

155–a none-too-impressive Parisian suburban neighborhood dressed-up with spring flowers and used as a setting for a *rencontre à trois:* Marcel, Robert, and Rachel

385–The charm and sadness of a site of *rencontre souhaitée et manquée* – where "quelques gouttes de pluie tombent sans bruit sur l'eau antique" and "après que les géraniums ont inutilement, en intensifiant l'éclairage de leurs couleurs, lutté contre le crépuscule assombri, une brume vient envelopper l'île qui s'endort; on se promène dans l'humide obscurité le long de l'eau où tout au plus le passage silencieux d'un cygne vous étonne..."

572–a glimpse of the roofs of Paris and an aggregate of houses seen through the Guermantes' courtyard

897–an *éperon de falaise,* spur, or lower outcropping of a sea cliff that temporarily hides the water

904–Proustian humor and Proustian scandal at an unappreciated sunset seen from these very cliffs mentioned immediately above–"Oui, c'est incomparable, dit légèrement Madame Verdurin, en jetant un coup d'oeil... et elle ramena son regard vers ses cartes."

1004–several pages of impressions of landscape seen from an automobile – and significant not only of Proust's very early attempts at descriptive journalism but of his various encounters with modern inventions that mark the flow of Time: the telephone, the automobile, the airplane

VOLUME III

9–weather and light rendered by the sounds of the street heard by Marcel in his room in Paris

116–138–the sounds of the Parisian streets, *les cris de Paris*

175–an interesting treatment of the play of two shadows, those of Marcel and Albertine

411–two pages of description of Parisian smells and their associative values, a study in synesthesia

623–627–the memorable description of Venice, a Venice "où les églises montaient de l'eau"

645–an important description of Saint-Mark's of Venice

762–just after pages that are unfortunately pessimistic and even sordid, a scene of brightness and beauty: the highly colored sky of Paris

Many critics have done justice to the floral beauty and possible message of the hawthorn *impression-description-appel* (I, 138). It is a recognized anthology piece, the last lines of which read:

Au haut des branches, comme autant de ces petits rosiers, aux pots cachés dans des papiers en dentelles dont aux grandes fêtes on faisait rayonner sur l'autel les minces fusées, pullulaient mille petits boutons d'une teinte plus pâle qui, en s'entr'ouvrant, laissaient voir, comme au fond d'une coupe de marbre rose, de rouges sanguines, et trahissaient, plus **encore** que les fleurs, l'essence particulière, irrésistible de l'épine, **qui** partout où elle bourgeonnait, où elle allait fleurir, ne le pouvait qu'en rose. Intercalé dans la haie, mais aussi différent d'elle qu'une jeune fille en robe de fête au milieu de personnes en négligé qui resteront à la maison, tout prêt pour le mois de Marie, dont il semblait faire partie déjà, tel brillait en souriant dans sa fraîche toilette rose l'arbuste catholique et délicieux. (I, 140)

In the passage just quoted Proust was carrying out ever so clearly his pronouncement in *Le Temps retrouvé* that "il prendra deux objets différents, posera leur rapport". We mean by this that he treated the hawthorns metaphorically and not merely descriptively. In this passage just quoted, the use of "jeune fille en robe de fête" and "coupe de marbre" enrich a natural description associated with a religious festival and not limited to a mere pictorial representation of a plant.

The hawthorn rencontre interests us further because it is one of the novel's early *appels* (sometimes called *impressions bienheureuses* by the author). Georges Cattaui describes Proust's particular contemplation of natural objects and their corresponding power of evocation in a passage that could refer equally well to the three trees of Hudimesnil or to the hawthorns of "Combray":

Comme une image détachée d'un rêve de la nuit, les choses—lorsqu'elles nous forcent à descendre en nous-mêmes, faisant notre esprit trébucher entre quelques années lointaines et l'heure présente—ces choses exercent sur notre âme leur puissance de suggestion: elles agissent à la façon d'une incantation. Et ce sont des symboles que deviennent pour le poète certains événements, certaines *rencontres*. Compagnons de notre enfance, amis disparus, invoquant de communs souvenirs, les choses-fantômes viennent à nous comme des ombres, nous demandant de 'les rendre à la vie'. Et dans 'leur gesticulation naïve et paissonnée', nous reconnaissons 'le regret, impuissant d'un être aimée qui a perdu l'usage de la parole...'[1]

Although the hawthorn experience may not have produced any degree of absolute revelation, it has at least broached the subject of the hidden appeal of plants: and, aesthetically, it is a splendid example of one of Proust's metaphorical passages. Within the order of plot development, it is of interest as a passage flanked by the Narrator's hoped-for meeting with Gilberte and her first appearance in "Combray".

The next impression chosen for analysis deals with the play of light:

Souvent le soleil se cachait derrière une nuée qui déformait son ovale et dont il jaunissait la bordure. L'éclat, mais non la clarté, était enlevé à la campagne où toute vie semblait suspendue, tandis que le petit village de Roussainville sculptait sur le ciel le relief de ses arêtes blanches avec une précision et un fini accablants. Un peu de vent faisait envoler un corbeau qui retombait dans le lointain, et contre le ciel blanchissant, le lointain des bois paraissait plus bleu, comme peint dans ces camaïeux qui décorent les trumeaux des anciennes demeures.[2]

First, the author has taken a simple subject for depiction – a *paysage moyen*,[3] no breath-taking splendor of nature but a relatively humble, homely, intimate, and quiet setting within that same general part of Europe that could inspire a Du Bellay in Anjou, a Ronsard in his Vendôme, a George Sand in her Berry, or Balzac in Touraine. Secondly, his technique of description is great enough to present to us all the reality of that fringe around a cloud-veiled sun's disk and to catch the play of color and light both around the "ovale" or "disque" and down upon the woods Méséglise-Way. This realism, however, is intensified for Proust's sympathetic

---

[1] Cattaui, *op. cit.*, p. 193.

[2] I, p. 150.

[3] Again we use the expression employed by Laumonier in conveying the appeal Vendôme had for Ronsard. Again we feel within Proust's spirit the charm that a gentle, simple, domestic, and 'domesticated' countryside held for him. He surely recognized what we term a "douceur beauceronne", one that parallels Du Bellay's "douceur angevine".

readers in that he has poetized the resultant forest color into "camaïeux qui décorent les trumeaux".

Thus, "Combray" has given us beautifully worded examples of an *impression-appel* (in the hawthorn description) and an *impression-description* (in the sun-woods scene just considered). If the 'call' of the former was somewhat fugitive, fleeting, and generally evasive, we cannot say that of the next rencontre chosen for examination: *la rencontre avec les clochers de Martinville.*

Let us recall briefly the incident of the three steeples of Martinville. Marcel had been riding one late afternoon in Dr. Percepied's carriage. In the countryside around Combray one enjoyed long views because of the sweeping plains. Marcel was impressed by a pair of church towers and then a third, isolated one in just such a distant view. Naturally, the towers' position changed for the viewer as the carriage moved along the country road. Once all three even converged. The Narrator was so much moved by this example of changing perspective achieved through motion that he felt the necessity of inditing his impressions. Consequently, we have at this point in "Combray" an example of the Narrator's response to an *appel* and an early and successful effort to write.

In analysing the incident, we must remember that the most fecund experiences of Proust and his Narrator were linked with the sensations of space.[4] They both were sensitive to distance, perspective, and movement in space. For example, the Narrator (on the northern coast of France in the cliff country) might have been on the top of an escarpment looking down, or at the foot of a cliff looking up with rapture. Or he was often confined to a room, the very dimensions of which were of concern to him. Or, as is true in the case in hand, he might be looking at three Martinville towers in changing perspective.

The very call of the above-mentioned steeples was conveyed to Marcel through a sunny surface which almost cried out that there was a mysterious essence to be found there. Then the steeples converged in an equally provocative phenomenon of linear vision.

[4]   Cattaui, *op. cit.*, p. 267.

This experience has introduced a number of themes:

(1) that minor theme of the presence of a second person on a carriage seat at the moment of a rencontre;[5]

(2) the theme of the inefficacy of intelligence in probing messages as sent out by these towers; the theme, on the other hand, of an intuitive force so strong that it "rips apart their bark-like surfaces";

(3) the theme of the will; for the urgency to indite his impressions is so great that the Narrator this time was strong enough to resist procrastination;

(4) the announcement of the artistic vocation; for this time Marcel has decided not merely to keep "en reserve dans ma tête des lignes remuantes au soleil";

(5) the theme of the use of the metaphor; because we have in the description of the steeples the poetic figures of three flowers and three girls; especially in the latter case, there is a definite relationship: the three towers in changing their perspective and then eventually grouping together at the very moment the sun is going down have reminded the Narrator of the legend of three girls lost at nightfall in a forest and forced to hover together; and surely they symbolize for us the very animation of inanimate objects.

Besides being a companion piece to the incident of the *pavés inégaux*, which experience (along with related ones at the end of the novel) also evoked the artistic vocation, this encounter with steeples was, then, literally bristling with themes: preoccupation with space, the search for the "essence" of inanimate objects, the discovery of such an essence within the Narrator himself, intuition versus intelligence, the artistic vocation, the use of the metaphor, the will, and the luxury of solitude and its relation to contemplation.

---

[5] Marcel was for a long time next to the coachman; but the latter's very uncommunicative nature was of value because Marcel's contemplation was not interrupted. In opposite situation (i.e., where the second person's presence prevented an encounter from becoming fruitful), Madame Villeparisis had kept Marcel from (a) grasping the full message of the three trees near Hudimesnil and (b) making successful advances towards a young girl he had sighted.

In the middle of *La Recherche*, again a drive inspired an impression. Riding with the Verdurins along the northern French coast, Marcel looked down upon the sea:

De la hauteur où nous étions déjà, la mer n'apparaissait plus, ainsi que de Balbec, pareille aux ondulations de montagnes souleveés, mais, au contraire, comme apparaît d'un pic, ou d'une route qui contourne la montagne, un glacier bleuâtre, ou une plaine éblouissante, situés à une moindre altitude. Le déchiquetage des remous y semblaient immobilisé et avoir dessiné pour toujours leurs cercles concentriques; l'émail même de la mer, qui changeait insensiblement de couleur, prenait vers le fond de la baie, où se creusait un estuaire, la blancheur bleue d'un lait où de petits bacs noirs qui n'avançaient pas semblaient empêtrés comme des mouches. Il ne me semblait pas qu'on pût découvrir un tableau plus vaste. Mais à chaque tournant une partie nouvelle s'y ajoutait, et quand nous arrivâmes à l'Octroi de Doville, l'éperon de falaise qui nous avait caché jusque-là une moitié de la baie rentra, et je vis tout à coup à ma gauche un golfe aussi profond que celui que j'avais eu jusque-là devant moi, mais dont il changeait les proportions et doublait la beauté. L'air à ce point si élevé devenait d'une vivacité et d'une pureté qui m'enivraient.[6]

After a reference to the Verdurins' indifference to the scene, which was, for them, little more than a setting for their all-important social life, the description goes on:

De l'octroi, la voiture s'étant arrêtée pour un instant à une telle hauteur au-dessus de la mer que, comme d'un sommet, la vue du gouffre bleuâtre donnait presque le vertige, j'ouvris le carreau; le bruit distinctement perçu de chaque flot qui se brisait avait, dans sa douceur et dans sa netteté, quelque chose de sublime. N'était-il pas comme un indice de mensuration qui, renversant nos impressions habituelles, nous montre que les distances verticles peuvent être assimilées aux distances horizontales, au contraire de la représentation que notre esprit s'en fait d'habitude; et que, rapprochant ainsi de nous le ciel, elles ne sont pas grandes; qu'elles sont même moins grandes pour un bruit qui les franchit, comme faisait celui de ces petits flots, car le milieu qu'il a à traverser est plus pur? Et, en effet, si on reculait seulement de deux mètres en arrière de l'octroi, on ne distinguait plus ce bruit de vagues auquel deux cents mètres de falaise n'avait pas enlevé sa délicate, minutieuse et douce précision.[7]

[6]   II, p. 897.
[7]   II, p. 898.

Such a descriptive passage is significant in that it:

(1) further develops the idea of space and perspective,

(2) forms in *La Recherche* the second and contrasting half of a diptych that embraces also the first impression of the sea at Balbec (I, 672), where the waters are a chain of mountains rather than a glacial plain,

(3) is excellent preparation for the passage on Madame Verdurin's indifference to natural beauty (II, 904),

(4) shows how the Narrator developed something of the same intoxication and tender emotion while over-drinking at the restaurant at Rivebelle (again an example of Proustian symmetry)

(5) shows how Proust presented not merely the object in descriptions but gave us his delightful subjective impressions of them.

It is clear that those vital zones, the Illiers-Combray country-side and the Northern Coast furnished Proust and his narrator an almost inexhaustible supply of subjects for descriptive writing that dealt with the natural scene. A third province, the city, now commands our attention.

In spite of the avowed general superiority of the Combray descriptions, the celebrated *cris de Paris*[8] in *La Prisonnière* are, in their own domain, examples of both brilliant writing and magnificent rencontres with sound. Those same rich themes of the awakening, the role of changing weather (an unseasonable and false spring, a pre-spring), in dead winter, and the use of sound to render color or light, all introduce a situation in which:

L'ouïe, ce sens délicieux, nous apporte la compagnie de la rue, dont elle nous retrace toutes les lignes, dessine toutes les formes qui y passent, nous en montrant la couleur.[9]

---

[8] Read over thirty years ago, it was the *cris de Paris* even more than "Combray", with all its natural beauty, that first aroused our interest in Proust's works. Some of his *correspondances*, such as Gregorian chanting heard through cries of 'artichokes', parallel the phenomenon of hearing (in the "Sabre Dance") traffic swinging up through mid- and upper-Manhattan.

[9] III, p. 116.

These impressions occur in that part of the novel where Albertine and Marcel are living together. Awakening one pre-spring morning, Marcel heard with particular interest many cries and street sounds of the city. Some, he found, had a definite correspondence with music. A vendor's cry of "artichokes" seemed to render Gregorian chanting. A passing automobile seemed to produce the harmonious sound of a violin. The "corne du tramway" and the "sifflet du marchand de tripes" suggested the pulse of light and heavy traffic. Can we not hear New York traffic in the "Sabre Dance"?

Some of the street cries that render "sensible la vie circulante des métiers, des nourritures de Paris" were associated with Albertine's own tastes. Even more important, these sounds symbolized that outer world, that scene of possible rencontres, in which the Narrator did not wish to lose his prisoner:

En plus du plaisir de savoir le goùt qu'Albertine avait pour eux et de sortir moi-même tout en restant couché, j'entendais en eux comme le symbole de l'atmosphère du dehors, de la dangereuse vie remuante au sein de laquelle je ne la laissais circuler que sous ma tutelle, dans un prolongement extérieur de la séquestration, et d'où je la retirais à l'heure que je voulais pour la faire rentrer auprès de moi.[10]

The cries of Paris functioned, then, as symbols. Furthermore, they have been presented not only in all their Parisian reality but also through apt poetic figures. They have once more shown Proust's forte for combining light and sound. In his interchangeable treatment of these two elements of physical life – light and sound – we can say that the literary result is double: production of both a resonant luminosity and a luminous resonance. We thus sense here the same type of beauty as in the synesthesia of the 'colored sounds' of the syllables of the name, Guermantes.

To summarize the subject of Proustian impressions, we next propose to discuss his techniques, to show the aesthetic value and plot significance of such descriptions, to connect Proust's writing with that of other literary schools, and finally, to bring into relief

[10]   III, p. 126.

what is most important to the sensitive reader: the intrinsic beauty
of descriptive writing in *La Recherche*.

Proust made particularly effective use of poetic figures that
could go from the humble to the elegant, or, inversely, from the
sublime to the homely. For an example of moving from the humble
to the elegant, we have but to witness, the change of none-too-
pretentious forest haze into a monochromatic bas-relief of some
castle (I, 150). An example of moving from the sublime to the
homely is the transposition of boats seen well below a majestic
cliff upon resplendent water into dark flies on whitish–blue milk
(II, 898).

In the many impressions throughout *La Recherche*, we have
observed three further Proustian techniques: delicate shading and
coloring, the resonance of luminosity, and, finally, a graceful
application of an acute sense of distance and contour.

Aesthetically, the impressions-rencontres have clearly served
these three purposes:

(1) As the reminiscences-rencontres they have often contributed to the
symmetry of the long novel.

(2) But often, too, they seem to appear from nowhere and to be without
distinct order, to be merely charming scenes coming unexpectedly
along a leisurely stroll.

(3) They have obviously furnished relief to the reader surfeited with
passages devoted to the movement of the world of people, the social
world. Or, for that matter, lengthy psychological ruminations in
La Recherche can often be 'diluted' thanks to a refreshing natural
scene of plants, light, or water.

Perhaps the greatest importance of many of these impressions
is that they serve as magical settings for actual encounters of
people. In reading certain brilliant descriptive passages in love
episodes, we are most aware of the *lieu de rencontre*, be it the Bois
de Boulogne for Madame de Stermaria or the coast near Balbec
for Albertine:

Je rentrai en pensant à cette matinée, en revoyant l'éclair au café
que j'avais fini de manger avant de me laisser conduire par Elstir auprès
d'Albertine, la rose que j'avais donnée au vieux monsieur, tous ces

détails choisis à notre insu par les circonstances et qui composent pour nous, en un arrangement spécial et fortuit, le tableau d'une première rencontre.[11]

Proust's writing seems to have distinct characteristics of various literary schools; sometimes his writing shows a fusion of literary schools and tenets. Edmund Wilson's *Axel's Castle* stresses the actual fusion or blending of naturalism and symbolism in Proust's work as well as in Joyce's. On the other hand, we sense in Proust's novels writing in which he announces and even attains surrealism.

Throughout the novel we note Proust's concern with the subconscious mind and his primary capacity for metamorphosing. And his world is often a symbolical one: Méséglise-Way represents the French bourgeoisie; Combray church is the equivalent of Time. His writing is marked often by fantasy. Nonetheless, he does write at times 'realistically' – in the simple, narrow, and earlier sense of the literary term, realism. For example, Balzac's ambition had been to make a certain amount of *rêve* with *du vrai*.[12] When Proust wrote in "Combray" of the end of the lilac season, he gave us a direct,[13] 'realistic' description of beautiful plants in the style of some nineteenth century writers:

Le temps des lilas approchait de sa fin; quelques-uns effusaient encore en hauts lustres mauves les bulles délicates de leurs fleurs, mais dans bien des parties du feuillage où déferlait, il y avait seulement une semaine, leur mousse embaumée, se flétrissait, diminuée et noirice, une écume creuse, sèche et sans parfum.[14]

A botanist, a nature-lover, or a generally observant person, upon reading "...noircie, une écume creuse, sèche...", surely recognizes here a very accurate description – remindful of some of

---

[11]   I, p. 874.
[12]   Such a result cannot be denied in the case of botanical descriptions in *Le Lys dans la vallée*, very direct and realistic descriptions of flowers that made an impression of great beauty, created an atmosphere of *rêve* within the framework of a *real* description.
[13]   'Direct' with one reservation – there is here, too, a possible metaphor: the lingering foam of a wave that has just broken on the strand.
[14]   I, p. 136.

the painstaking delineations of the literature of the nineteenth century.

We can say that Proust's genius resides in part in just such a return to the style of an earlier period. Such a *retour* amid passages of challenging modernity shows how well Proust seemed to link the twentieth century with the preceding one.

As a further example, along with a Venice[15] where "la lumière qui s'attarde sur les canaux . . . semble une dernière note longuement tenue par quelque pédale optique",[16] there can be on the other hand 'realistic', straightforward descriptions of a landscape, or a room, of the language (including slang) peculiar to a certain individual or to a special social group. Such injections serve to give relief and depth to other passages that abound in the metaphor or the subjective impressions of Proust. This fusion helps *La Recherche* to attain the very greatest degree of reality.

The rencontres-reminiscences with inaminate objects or natural forces often revealed a philosophical message without being necessarily beautiful. The impressions as rencontres merely hinted on occasion at a philosophical message but were in themselves most beautiful. This intrinsic beauty of Proust's descriptions is a focal point within this chapter division. Their charm and excellence excite genuine aesthetic pleasure.

Rencontres-reminiscences with the inanimate served to 'regain Time' for Proust. They finally revealed to him that their 'essence' was not really within themselves. It was within the viewer himself. Such a *moi*, in Proust's case (and the Narrator's), would attain expression through writing. Thus rencontres-reminiscences have inspired rencontres-impressions. These latter are the most significant results of the whole experience of 'regained Time'. In incomparable words, in brilliant impressionistic-descriptive writing, Proust has painted the setting for his recaptured past.

Proust was able to picture the natural scene in such a way that we could view the sea, feel the seasons, or appreciate the

---

[15]   It is interesting to note, in passing, that this is just the opposite of the situation of light reproduced by sound at Combray (I, 83).

[16]   Jean Pommier, *La Mystique de Marcel Proust*, p. 48.

French countryside through his eyes, that we could look upon things around us in a way different from our customary one. Proust had an unusual capacity for adding a subjective impression to the object itself. A botanical description serves as an example of such writing. We note here how he has re-created, one of those places with its "empire particulier", where nature consummates man's work – a pond scene on a French estate.

C'est ainsi qu'au pied de l'allée qui dominait l'étang artificiel, s'était composée sur deux rangs, tressés de fleurs de myosotis et de pervenches, la couronne naturelle, délicate et bleue qui ceint le front clair-obscur des eaux, et que le glaïeul, laissant fléchir ses glaives avec un abandon royal, étendait sur l'eupatoire et la grenouillette au pied mouillé les fleurs de lis en lambeaux, violettes et jaunes, de son sceptre lacustre.[17]

This eloquent bit of testimony shows us that Proust's aesthetic calling had for a primary function the expression of natural beauty as experienced and interpreted by man.

[17]   I, p. 136.

5

CONCLUSION

Such a march of rencontres with the inanimate has been most varied and instructive. We propose to show how they have served as vehicles of the following themes and mediums of the following functions:

(1) chance, and chance as opposed to necessity,
(2) mobility and immobility as aesthetic-ethical ideas,
(3) art as a vocation,
(4) sheer joy and pleasure,
(5) plot-development,
(6) natural beauty and appeal,
(7) the time-effacing value of *La Recherche*.

CHANCE. – Throughout *La Recherche* the Narrator has stumbled upon impressive scenes or quite unexpectedly heard meaningful sounds. Throughout this booklet we have underlined the fortuitous character of these and similar sensory experiences.

In *Le Temps retrouvé* we found first a Narrator who could be described as someone believing in a "plan of abstract 'laws' that determine or control a ridiculous world constantly in movement."[1] In the series of revelations beginning with the experience of the *pavés inégaux*, though, a wonderful play of chance revealed to him that:

Dans le monde d'universelle relativité et d'universel écoulement auquel il appartient, s'est donc construit, un monde absolu, au hasard

---

[1] Brée, *op. cit.*, p. 41.

d'une vie individuelle, découvert aussi par le hasard de sensations individuelles, et qui par suite échappe doublement à toute nécessité.[2]

While there is a great deal of order and determinism in Proust's world, there is no truly planned, Aristotelian rencontre with natural objects but rather a magical injection of chance. Insisting upon the involuntary nature[3] of Proust's experiences, Robert Champigny goes so far as to say, "Et puis c'est le hasard qui chez Proust semble régir..."[4] Proust's experiences with the inanimate have been privileged in that it is not effort and pure necessity that have brought them about. Chance has performed the miracle.

MOBILITY AND IMMOBILITY. – The opposition of mobility and immobility is as interesting as that of chance and necessity. Paradoxically enough, Proust wishes to eliminate the immobility and immutability of things themselves; yet he wishes at the same time to check the mobility of a world of movement and change. Let us simplify this idea of a need for artistic 'mobility' on the one hand and for philosophical immobility on the other hand:

As a writer, he wished to eliminate the immobility and immutability of things. He wished to render them as Elstir did — ever changing, alive, part of himself, and subject to impressions themselves. He wished to "dissoudre les choses",[5] almost to give animation to inaminate objects,[6] and finally, to capture their essence. This latter accomplishment is the capital rencontre of all: *sa propre rencontre.*

---

[2]   *Ibid.*, p. 52.

[3]   Whether this insistence on chance and "le caractère involontaire" of experiences is what Robert Champigny terms a "coquetterie mystique" is a question for the metaphysicians to decide. As stated in our introduction, we do not propose to treat the encounter philosophically, asking and attempting to answer such an astounding question as, "How and why do encounters come about?".

[4]   Robert Champigny, "Temps et Reconnaissance chez Marcel Proust," *PMLA*, Mar 1958, p. 133.

[5]   Claude-Edmonde Magny, *Les Sandales d'Empédocle*, p. 154.

[6]   Not too far removed from Sartre's experiences and aspirations in *La Nausée.*

As a philosopher, he was ever confronted with the phenomenon of movement and change in the world and of transformation of people, either through physical ravages of time or through personality evolution. To combat this movement is the achieved immobility of *un peu de temps à l'état pur*. This immobility can be eternity as in the case of the *petite phrase*, the *pavés inégaux* and accompanying azure, the boat sounds off Balbec.

This eternity, along with the first-mentioned 'mobility' of things that liberated their essence, must be rendered artistically.

ART AS A VOCATION. – Everywhere *La Recherche* hints at the hidden appeal of things. Throughout we fall upon suggestions of the vocation to be revealed. The Narrator was forever preoccupied with such a search for truth and beauty:

> Que ce soit pour faire sien le secret des clochers, des arbres ou des aubépines, que ce soit pour faire sortir d'une sensation le passé qu'elle cache et qu'elle contient, ne s'agit-il pas aussi bien dans l'un et l'autre cas de dégager une existence, une vérité, une beauté 'à demi pressenties, à demi incompréhensibles, dont la compréhension est le but vague, mais permanent' de la pensée du narrateur.[7]

Memory, if not the vocation, was evoked by the madeleine experience. The incident of the steeples of Martinville materialized a partial revelation of the narrator's calling. The hawthorns and the three trees of Hudimesnil urged him on. The series of experiences of involuntary memory during the "Matinée at the Guermantes" are a consummate victory.

JOY AND PLEASURE. – Rencontres with the inanimate produced sheer joy and pleasure for the Narrator: Such delight in beauty was conspicuous in the early passages of the novel, where he spoke so eloquently of perfumes, the echo of a step on a gravel path, or the evaporating bubble on a pond's surface. All this formed part of his "sol mental":

> C'est parce que je croyais aux choses, aux êtres, tandis que je les parcourais, que les choses, les êtres qu'ils m'ont fait connaître sont les seuls que je prenne encore au sérieux et qui me donnent encore de la joie.[8]

---

[7] Léon Guichard, *Introduction à la lecture de Marcel Proust*, p. 44.
[8] I, p. 184.

He spoke again of the same joys (as well as of the hidden vocation) in the middle of the novel (II, 397, and II, 1126). Finally he told us that "les paradis perdus" (III, 870) form the true Paradise. Genuine joy has been experienced through a past captured by meetings with the inanimate.

PLOT DEVELOPMENT. – Léon Guichard treats of the "triple fonction" of chance sensations. The first of these results or functions is the actual pleasure described above, whereas the last is the actual construction of the book:

> D'abord, elles [Les sensations fortuites] sont en elles-mêmes un plaisir; ...elles constituent pour le narrateur le seul plaisir possible: celui qu'on goûte en revivant le passé dans le présent, dans l'anéantissement du Temps, ou dans l'appréhension du Temps à l'état pur... et c'est leur troisième fonction qui nous intéresse maintenant. Dans la construction même de l'oeuvre d'art, elles vont servir au romancier.[9]

Rencontres with people have naturally developed the plot. A snowball of *rencontres* comes from the initial meeting with Swann. Inspiration springs from the meetings and relations with Bergotte, Elstir, and Vinteuil. On the other hand, particular rencontres with inanimate objects (if we rearrange the order of the book or somewhat reverse the rôles of Proust and his narrator) have inspired just such writing – as seen in this vast novel.

Meetings with the inanimate have shown themselves of further plot significance in that they (1) have been somewhat associated with plot characters, (2) have served as *lieux de rencontre* for characters, and (3) have served as symbols and symmetry-producing mooring-points.

NATURE. – Proust's *La Recherche* reveals a vibrant response to natural beauty. We have noted that his vital rencontres were never with animals, but he has captured all the appeal of a plant, from shimmering leaves to multi-colored blossoms. He has recognized the compelling glow of the sky and the bewitching roll of the sea. He has added grace to the already appealing contours of the forested hills of northern France. The cliffs, orchards, river-

---

[9]   Guichard, *op. cit.*, p. 41.

banks, sunsets, lilac bushes, aquatic plants, fluctuations of light, and tremulous ivy he met and described could not fail to be significant and impelling rencontres for one with his sensitivity.

TIME-EFFACING VALUE. – Proust and his narrator were not satisfied with viewing beauty alone, with looking wide-eyed upon the natural appeal of land and sea, with gratifying a mere aesthetic-sensualistic pleasure. They were to go further, to combat time through such sunsets, plants, echoes, and perfumes:

Souffrant, non moins que Joubert, de n'avoir qu'une existence temporelle, spatiale, successive, toujours séparée par la distance et la limite de l'objet dont elle veut jouir, Proust, afin de se delivrer de cette obsession, fait en sorte que chaque instant de l'existence soit par lui chargé d'un écho, d'un parfum, d'une dimension. Ecrivant avec un sentiment épuré de la mémoire, avec l'espace et la perspective du souvenir, il a mis son génie dans sa sensibilité.[10]

Marcel Proust expresses in *La Recherche* somewhat the same idea more succinctly:

Une heure n'est pas une heure, c'est un vase rempli de parfums, de sons, de projets, et de climats.[11]

Time has been captured thanks to inanimate objects. Next the captured essence of things and the victory over Time must be expressed as literature. Temporal permanence, such an excellent answer to man's condition of 'nothingness' and 'non-being' is thus established:

Proust pénètre 'jusqu'à la grande nuit impénétrée et décourageante de notre âme – que nous prenons pour du vide et du néant'; et voici que, du sein de cette nuit, véritable voyant, notre nocturne Marcel nous donne *le pressentiment de ces mystères qui n'ont sans doute leur explication que dans d'autres mondes;* et, quoique incroyant, il nous apporte, à sa façon – qui est celle du poète et non celle du mystique – la preuve qu'il existe autre chose que le néant.[12]

---

10 Cattaui, *op. cit.*, p. 197.
11 III, p. 889.
12 Cattaui, *op. cit.*, p. 254.

La Recherche has shown itself to be a novel that appeals to those of all beliefs and to those without beliefs. Not really as a mystic, but as an artist, Proust, through his rencontres, has brushed aside the *néant*. He was a forerunner of André Malraux, who would do the same thing through plastic art, photography, architecture, or writing:

Le plus grand mystère n'est pas que nous soyons jetés au hasard entre la profusion de la matière et celle des astres; c'est que, dans cette prison, nous tirions de nous-mêmes des images assez puissantes pour nier notre néant.[13]

An artistic *vocation* had sprung from an *appel* and revelation, which, in turn, was a *chance* sensation derived from a fortuitous encounter, a *rencontre* with natural forces and things.

[13]   André Malraux, *Les Noyers de l'Altenburg*, p. 243.

BIBLIOGRAPHY

Beckett, Samuel, *Proust* (New York, Grove Press, 1931).

Bell, Clive, *Marcel Proust* (London, Hogarth Press, 1928).

Bonnet, Henri, *Le Progrès spirituel dans l'oeuvre de Marcel Proust* (Paris, Librarie Philosophique J. Vrin, 1946).

Brée, Germaine, *Du Temps perdu au Temps retrouvé* (Paris, Société Edition 'Les Belles Lettres', 1950).

Brée, Germaine, *Marcel Proust and Deliverance from Time* (New York, Grove Press, 1955).

Bret, Jacques, *Marcel Proust* (Geneva, Edition du Mont-Blanc, 1946).

Cattaui, Georges, *L'Amitié de Proust* (Paris, Gillimard, 1935) (Volume VIII of *Les Cahiers Marcel Proust.)*

Cattaui, Georges, *Marcel Proust* (Paris, Julliard, 1952).

Champigny, Robert, "Temps et Reconnaissance chez Proust", *PMLA*, March, 1958.

Clark, Charles N., "Love and Time: The Erotic Imagery of Marcel Proust", *Yale French Studies*, Number 11.

Cordle, Thomas H., "Dreams in *A la Recherche du Temps perdu*", *Romantic Review*, Volume 42 (December, 1951).

Crémieux, Benjamin, *Du Côté de Marcel Proust* (Paris, Editions Lemarget, 1929).

Curtius, Ernst Robert, *Französischer Geist im zwanzigsten, Jahrhundert* (Bern, Francke, 1952).

Fernandez, Ramon, Preface of *Les Cahiers Marcel Proust* II (Paris, Gallimard, 1928).

Feuillerat, Albert, *Comment Marcel Proust a composé son roman* (New Haven, Yale University Press, 1934).

François, Simone, *Le Dandyisme et Marcel Proust* Chapter II, "Une Rencontre de Marcel Proust" (Bruxelles, Palais des Académies, 1956).

Gramont, Elisabeth de, *Marcel Proust* (Flammarion, Paris, 1948).

Green, F. M., *The Mind of Proust* (Cambridge University Press, 1949).

Guichard, Léon, *Introduction à la lecture de Marcel Proust* (Paris, Nizet, 1956).

Hier, Florence, *La Musique dans l'oeuvre de Marcel Proust* (New York, Publications of the Institute of French Studies, 1933).

Hindus, Molton, *The Proustian Vision* (New York, Columbia University, 1954).

Hommage à Marcel Proust (Paris, Gallimard, 1927) (Volume I of *Les Cahiers Marcel Proust*).

Jauss, Hans R., *Zeit und Erinnerung in Marcel Proust A LA RECHERCHE DU TEMPS PERDU* (Heidelberg, Universitätsverlag, 1955).

Kneller, John W., "The Musical Structure of Proust's "Un Amour de Swann", *Yale French Studies*, Number 4.

Kolb, Philip, *La Correspondance de Marcel Proust* (Urbana, University of Illinois Press, 1949).

Le Figaro, July 23, 1907.

Leon, Derrick, *Introduction to Proust* (London, Kegan Paul, 1940).

Louria, Yvette, *La Convergence stylistique chez Proust* (Geneva, Librairie E. Droz, 1957).

Magny, Claude-Edmonde, *Les Sandales d'Empedocle* (Boudry, Switzerland, Edition de la Branconnière, 1945).

Malraux, André, *Les Noyers de l'Altenburg* (Paris, Gallimard, 1948).

Mansfield, Lester, *Le Comique dans l'oeuvre de Proust* (Paris, 1952).

March, Harold, *The Two Worlds of Marcel Proust* (Philadelphia, University of Pennsylvania Press, 1948).

Mauriac, François, *Proust's Way* (New York, Philosophical Library, 1951).

Maurois, André, Preface, *A la Recherche du Temps perdu*, Volume I (Paris, Gallimard, Edition de la Pléiade, 1954).

Maurois, André, *A la Recherche de Marcel Proust* (Paris, Hachette, 1949).

Miller, Milton M., M. D., *Nostalgia: A Psychoanalytical Study of Marcel Proust* (Boston, Houghton-Mifflin, 1956).

Mouton, Jean, *Le Style de Marcel Proust* (Paris, Ed. Correa, 1948).

Pierre-Quint, Léon, *Marcel Proust, sa vie, son oeuvre* (Paris, Edition du Sagittaire, 1946).

Pommier, Jean, *La Mystique de Proust* (Paris, Droz, 1939).

Proust, Marcel, *A la Recherche du Temps perdu* (Paris, Gallimard, Edition de la Pléiade, 3 volumes, 1954).

Proust, Marcel, *Contre Sainte-Beuve* (Paris, Gallimard, 1954).

Proust, Marcel, *Jean Santeuil* (Paris, Gallimard, 1952), 3 volumes.

Proust, Marcel, *Les Plaisirs et les jours* (Paris, Gallimard, 1928).

Proust, Marcel, *Pastiches et mélanges* (Paris, Gallimard, 1919).

Remacle, Madeleine, *L'Element poétique dans A LA RECHERCHE DU TEMPS PERDU* (Bruxelles, Palais des Académies, 1954).

Souday, Paul, *Marcel Proust* (Paris, Kra, 1927).

INDEX

Aesthetic pleasure, 6, 15, 73, 77—78
Appels, 6, 16—17, 19, 40, 64, 67, 77, 80
Artistic vocation, 5, 22, 29—30, 40, 42, 44, 58—59, 66, 77, 80
Association, 13, 18, 26, 28, 35, 37, 39, 42, 44—45, 48—49, 70, 78
Authentic (involuntary) memory, 5, 20, 36, 42, 77

Blossoms, 22—23, 31—37, 61
Books, 20, 27, 53, 56—57

Chance:
  as opposed to necessity, 75—76
  its role in the novel, 36—37, 40—41, 51, 56, 59, 75—76, 80—81
Change, 34, 37—38, 40—41
Churches, 28—29, 32, 46—47, 61, 63
Cliffs, 63, 66, 68—69
Correspondances in the sense of Baudelaire, 18, 69

Descriptions:
  as result of impressions, 14, 61—74
  as result of reminiscences, 14, 61—67
  in plot development, 14, 61—74

Encounters (See Rencontres)
Essence of things, 14, 66—67, 73, 76

Forest haze, 15, 71

Habit, 38—39
Hawthorns, 17, 18, 22, 64
Hints at and rejection of mysticism, 6, 17, 32—33, 35—36, 54, 62, 66, 80

Imagination, 43—45, 55
Impressions:
  definition of, 17
  with descriptions, 60—74
Impressions bienheureuses, 17, 64
Inanimate (See Rencontres)
Inanimate forces, 29, 36
Intelligence, 51, 55
Intermittenc(i)es of the heart, 49—51
Involuntary (authentic) memory, 5, 20, 36, 42, 54, 77

Joy, 5—6, 15, 33, 77—78

Light, 24, 39, 65, 69—70

Madeleine, 17, 21, 36
Memory:
  general references, 40, 47, 73, 77
  involuntary (authentic) 5, 20, 36, 42, 54, 77
Metaphor, use of the, 18, 64, 67, 73
Metempsychosis, 6, 33
Miscellaneous inanimate objects, 28—30
Mobility and immobility as aesthetic-ethical ideas, 76—77

Moi, rencontres of the, 7, 14, 42, 47, 76

Moments identiques, 17, 54, 59

Moments privilégiés (See *Moments identiques*)

Music, 24—25, 28, 42, 49, 77

Names, 26—27, 53

Nature and natural beauty, 5—6, 15—16, 48, 60—61, 69, 73—74, 78—79

Odors, 26, 41—43

Places, 27—28, 45—49, 60

Plot Development, 8, 37, 41, 45, 48, 49, 59, 60, 65, 78

Reality, 34, 43—44, 45, 47—48, 53, 73

Reminiscences:
  definition of, 17
  rencontres as reminiscences, 20—59

Rencontre:
  as revelation, 14—15, 51, 77, 80
  definition of, 6—7
  discouraging and encouraging, 19, 48—49, 51—52, 53
  of people, 7, 14, 37, 71, 78
  of the *moi*, 7, 14, 42, 47, 50, 58, 73, 76
  places of or *"lieux de"* rencontres, 71—72, 78

Rencontre rêvée, souhaitée, désirée, cherchée, 7, 24, 28—38, 43, 48—49

Rencontres with the inanimate:
  blossoms, 22—23, 31—37, 61
  forest haze, 15, 71
  hawthorns, 17—18, 22, 64
  madeleine, 17, 21, 36
  names, 26—27, 43—45, 53

odors, 26, 41—43
places, 27—28, 45—49, 60
shrubs, 22—23, 31—37, 61
sounds, 24—26, 41—43
Towers of Martinville, 17, 66—67
trees, 22—23, 30, 31—37, 61
uneven paving-stones, 20, 54—55, 59
weather, 24, 37—41

Rooms and their role, 22, 66

Sea, 28, 60, 62, 68

Self-encounter (See Rencontre of the *moi*)

Shrubs, 22—23, 31—37, 61

Sounds, 24—26, 41—43

Space, sensations of, 32, 66, 69

Street-vendors, cries of, 63, 69—70

Subjective impressions, 52, 74, 76

Subjective reality (See Rencontres of the *moi*)

Symbols, 34, 37, 40, 42, 43, 45—49, 57, 70

Synesthesia, 18, 24, 30, 61, 63, 69—70

Temporal permanence, 8, 33—35, 58, 79

Time:
  chronological, 58, 63, 77
  dominated, 58, 79
  general references, 58, 63, 79
  lost, 77
  regained, 58, 73, 79

Towers of Martinville, 17, 66—67

Trees, 22—23, 30, 31—37, 61

Uneven paving-stones, 20, 54—55, 59

Weather, 24, 37—41

Will, 55, 57, 67

IISS Annual
Conference Papers

ADELPHI PAPERS

NUMBER ONE HUNDRED AND NINETY–NINE

S0-GQG-872

New Technology and Western Security Policy

Part III

THE INTERNATIONAL INSTITUTE FOR STRATEGIC STUDIES
23 TAVISTOCK STREET LONDON WC2E 7NQ

ADELPHI PAPER No. 199

The Papers contained in this Adelphi Paper and in Nos 197 and 198 were first presented to the 1984 IISS Annual Conference held in the Palais des Papes, Avignon, from 13th to 16th September 1984. They have been amended and revised as appropriate in light of discussion and comment at the Conference.

First published Summer 1985

ISBN 0 86079 090 8
ISSN 0567-932X

© The International Institute for Strategic Studies 1985

All rights reserved. No part of this publication may be reproduced, stored in a retrieval system, or transmitted in any form or by any means, electronic, mechanical, photo-copying, recording or otherwise, without the prior permission of the International Institute for Strategic Studies.

The International Institute for Strategic studies was founded in 1958 as a centre for the provision of information on and research into the problems of international security, defence and arms control in the nuclear age. It is international in its Council and staff, and its membership is drawn from over fifty countries. It is independent of governments and is not the advocate of any particular interest.

The Institute is concerned with strategic questions – not just with the military aspects of security but with the social and economic sources and political moral implications of the use and existence of armed force: in other words with the basic problems of peace.

The Institute's publications are intended for a much wider audience than its own membership and are available to the general public on subscription or singly.

Printed in Great Britain by Spottiswoode Ballantyne Ltd., Colchester

3.00P

CONTENTS

NEW TECHNOLOGY AND INTRA-ALLIANCE RELATIONSHIPS: NEW
STRENGTHS, NEW STRAINS   1

HON. DAVID M. ABSHIRE
*US Permanent Representative to the North Atlantic
Council, Brussels*

DEFENCE RESEARCH AND DEVELOPMENT AND WESTERN INDUSTRIAL
POLICY: PART I   15

PROF. SIR RONALD MASON
*Professor of Chemistry, University of Sussex, and formerly
Chief Scientific Adviser to Ministry of Defence, London*

DEFENCE RESEARCH AND DEVELOPMENT AND WESTERN INDUSTRIAL
POLICY: PART II   19

HENRI MARTRE
President and Director General, SNIAS, Paris

THE 'STAR WARS' DEBATE: THE WESTERN ALLIANCE AND STRATEGIC
DEFENCE: PART I   25

Marina-del-Rey, California

HE WESTERN ALLIANCE AND STRATEGIC
. . . .   34

Kings's College, University of

. . . .   51

stitute for Strategic Studies,

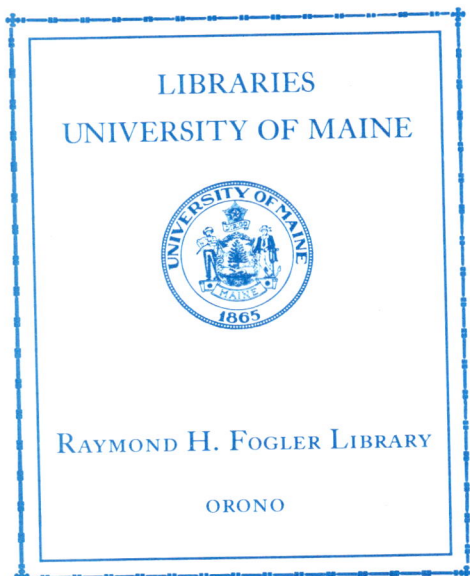

LIBRARIES
UNIVERSITY OF MAINE

RAYMOND H. FOGLER LIBRARY

ORONO

New Technology and Intra-Alliance Relationships: New Strengths, New Strains

HON. DAVID M. ABSHIRE

Introduction

One of the greatest challenges confronting the Atlantic Alliance today is managing the relationship between technological change and the other pieces of the military mosaic embracing leadership, tactics, logistics and strategy. The question is not whether technology can make a difference to NATO and to the Warsaw Pact; it will. It is not whether the nations of the Alliance and the Pact will use new technology; they are sure to. The issue is whether the Alliance will use technology in the most effective way possible. This Paper focuses on the relationship between change and NATO's conventional forces.

NATO's conventional forces are more important today than ever before. The weight and momentum of relentless Soviet force improvements in strategic and tactical nuclear forces as well as in conventional forces, threatens the credibility of NATO's strategy of flexible response. Flexible response remains a good strategy, but it must be made truly flexible, especially at the conventional level. Intensified popular concern over nuclear weapons demands that the nuclear threshold be raised. Both of these concerns can be met by improved conventional forces.

The need to improve NATO's conventional forces is also a transatlantic political imperative. The proposed Nunn–Roth Amendment to the FY 85 Military Authorization Bill focused on the shortfalls in NATO's conventional posture and called upon NATO allies to meet their commitments to force sustainability or face American troop withdrawals. Although the Amendment was ultimately defeated, the congressional debate underlined an issue that is likely to be the source of continuing political friction within the Alliance if nothing is done to remedy the problem.

Fortunately, the Alliance has the opportunity to use new technologies to improve the performance of its conventional forces, enhance deterrence and thereby promote the Alliance's fundamental goal of preserving peace.

New technologies are also creating opportunities for innovative operational concepts, revised doctrines and new tactics that will help NATO make flexible response truly flexible. Military commanders have long desired to do certain things that technology can now make possible.

While NATO can derive great strength from technology, technology can also create strains. An incredibly rapid pace of technological change confronts Alliance decision-makers with an enormous range of possible options. The stakes and risks associated with their decisions are high. So are the costs – a major difficulty at a time when the Alliance's economic resources are limited. Inevitably that combination produces strains.

These strains are exacerbated by unease within the Alliance that the dream made possible by new technology could become a nightmare in which the opponent exploits the same technologies available to the Alliance while NATO drags its heels in getting helpful technology into the field only to have its conventional forces overwhelmed.

NATO can meet the difficult and complex challenge of managing technological change in the military sphere. Of course, there will be problems along the way. In my judgment, NATO already has mechanisms to put new technology to best use and to reduce some of the inevitable strains. What is needed is an overall strategy to tie its decisions together as well as the leadership, vision and will to implement the strategy and to make that strategy work.

1

One must be clear about what one means by 'technology' in the NATO context. ET – 'emerging technologies' – has become a buzz-word in the Alliance. Unfortunately, the term 'emerging technologies' has not been used precisely but has been used to describe a confusing range of technological developments.

In fact, a three-part distinction can be drawn. *Operational* and *emerged* technology would be used during this decade in weapons projects that incorporate existing or maturing technologies. *Emerging* technology focuses on developing and producing improved conventional weapons for initial fielding throughout the 1990s. *Exploratory* technologies are those that are not yet mature but are potentially useful in projects 15 to 20 years in the future. Emerging technologies emphasize a longer term focus on research and development programmes for weapons that are not yet defined.

A second distinction is also helpful, that is, whether the new technology is introduced as a component to an existing system, or whether it develops as a subsystem or as an entire system on its own.

As an illustration of this point, laser technology exists, having already arrived on the battlefield in fire control ranging for fourth generation Main Battle Tanks. Over the next decade, it may emerge from this passive role to the point where a low power laser is actively used from existing platforms against opposing forces. By the turn of the century, there may be self-contained battlefield laser systems that are as identifiable and common as a main battle tank or tactical aircraft. Thinking about this system, let alone about the force structure, logistics and tactics that might surround it, is still undefined and, thus, it is still in the exploratory phase.

The current debate about technology's contribution to Western deterrence must keep these distinctions clear. In evaluating current NATO thinking and planning, for example, some analysts have exaggerated the exploratory nature of the technology under consideration. In fact, NATO is first focusing on exploiting newly *emerged* technologies. If there is a debate on the utility of such plans it should not be decided on the basis of such distortion but on an understanding of the real situation.

Managing Change And Changing Management

For the NATO alliance the key question is how to manipulate that change so that the conventional balance in Europe can be significantly improved. Over its last 35 years, NATO has shown a great capability to incorporate technological changes into its defence capabilities. Unpredictable, uncontrolled change, however, has caused problems and has made the Allies uncomfortable. It is at those times that Alliance relations suffer most.

As one thinks about NATO's technological potential and how well the Alliance will do in incorporating new technology, three questions must be addressed:

– Can one be satisfied with the way the Alliance has handled technology in the recent past?
– What has the Alliance learned about new technology that will prove useful as it looks to the future? What lessons should not be forgotten?
– Does the nature of new technology suggest the need for new approaches or modification of existing institutions and processes?

A Look at the Recent Past

The extent to which NATO members have been able to develop, share and incorporate technology into their common defence is a cause for justifiable pride. Nevertheless, a review of the recent record shows that NATO must do better if it is effectively to exploit its superior technological resources to strengthen its conventional forces. Several factors give cause for concern.

The Decline of Western Technological Superiority

In the early 1970s there was clear evidence of NATO's technological superiority across the conventional spectrum. A decade later, NATO can no longer make that claim. The Warsaw Pact is closing the technological gap at an alarming rate – to the point that the threat can increasingly be described in qualitative as well as quantitative terms. If this sounds alarmist, consider the following areas in which

NATO prided itself for a substantial lead 10 years ago:

- Special 'Chobham'-type armour;
- Second-generation guidance on anti-tank guided missiles;
- Artillery sub-munitions;
- Target acquisition and fire control;
- High energy/manoeuvrability aircraft;
- All aspects of air-to-air missiles and air-to-surface precision guided munitions;
- Multispectrum electronic counter-measures;
- Submarine design.

In each of these areas NATO may still have major advantages in the laboratory. In the last decade, however, the Warsaw Pact has virtually matched NATO in getting these technologies to the field. In short, the Alliance has had problems in translating its technological prowess into operational capability.

A Vicious Production Cycle
There are many reasons to explain the erosion of Western technological superiority in certain key areas. One that must be considered is that NATO asks more of its technology than the Warsaw Pact. NATO requires not only that its weapons keep pace with those of the Pact but that the quality of its weapons be sufficiently high to offset quantitative inferiority. At times this requirement has produced a vicious circle:

- Pushing quality requires taking greater risks with unproven, adolescent technology;
- Trying to capitalize on such technology results in frequent re-design and programmatic delays;
- Changing requirements and slowing programmes generate higher costs;
- Increasing costs produce lower unit buys with stretched and inefficient production rates, adding even higher costs and later delivery;
- Higher costs and later deliveries get fewer systems into the field;
- Fewer systems in the field drive the need to push quality and take even greater technological risks.

This phenomenon has created the danger of what defence analyst Thomas Callaghan

has called 'structural disarmament' – fewer and fewer systems for more and more money.[1] The Alliance should recognize that at some point numbers count no matter how good the technology.

Inventory Modernization
In contrast to NATO's earlier performance, the last decade has witnessed a disturbing trend in which each new generation of technology coming to the field represents a declining percentage of the Alliance's total inventory. There has also been a growing differentiation among Alliance members in the technological sophistication of the majority of their forces. If this trend continues, NATO could become a three-part Alliance with respect to technology – the US far outstripping the other Allies in the technological capabilities of her forces; a group of Allies with some 'cutting edge' technology and a large inventory of less capable systems; and all the rest who cannot afford to play a significant role in the high-technology game.

Technology Leakage
If one of the reasons for NATO's diminished technological superiority has been its problems in translating technological prowess into operational capability, another significant factor has been the persistent leakage of the latest advances to the Eastern Bloc. The examples of the Soviet acquisition of Western technology – legally or illegally – are numerous. The Soviet SA-7 heat seeking, shoulder-fired anti-air missile contains many features of the US *Redeye*. More than one-third of all known Soviet integrated circuits have been copied from US designs. Today, Western visitors to Soviet machine tool factories have been surprised if not shocked to see the very latest technologies – three-axis industrial robots, and diamond, boron nitride and ceramic-coded tooling.[2] There is something wrong when the Warsaw Pact gets the West's latest technology faster than the NATO allies.

Avoiding Damaging Fallacies
NATO's last thirty-five years and the historical evolution of technology should not be forgotten by the Atlantic Alliance as it

comes to grips with the exploitation of accelerating technological change. A look into the past might identify four warnings:

Avoid technology as 'the only answer'. Effective defence cannot be achieved by technology alone. Other dimensions are also critical. In the pursuit of technological advantage, one runs the risk of forgetting that technology is only one element of a nation's or an alliance's armed forces. It may not even be the most critical element. The conflict in the Falklands, the military encounters in the Middle East and a series of other examples suggest, in fact, that the human dimension remains paramount in determining the outcome of conflict.[3] No technology has been able to overcome fully the elements of the unexpected, chance or human ineptitude, irrationality, fear and confusion, that make up what Clausewitz so aptly labelled the fog of war. Only human leadership, and tactical and strategic ability, can cope with that.

Avoid the fallacy that technology substitutes for logistic inadequacy. Another set of factors that often gets overshadowed by the fascination with technology relates to readiness and sustainability. It makes litle difference how good an army's guns are if there is insufficient ammunition. Similarly, sophisticated aircraft are of little use if they are unable to operate from vulnerable airfields.

The readiness and sustainability of NATO's forces must be improved. Many of the readiness and sustainability measures that NATO should implement are relatively inexpensive. Unfortunately, undefended by powerful legislative constituencies or military and industrial lobbies, these measures tend to be the first areas sacrificed by budget cutters contending with limited resources. The issue is not one of an either/or choice between new technology and readiness and sustainability. Rather it is the question of the balance between the two. A weakness in combat posture undermines NATO's potential to defend early and forward and therefore defeats the purpose of costly efforts to improve sustainability. On the other hand, if the Alliance support posture is weak, combat capabilities will eventually be seriously degraded, even-

tually to the point where units can no longer operate effectively.

Avoid technology as an 'uninformed answer'. Technology must be exploited in the context of appropriate operational concepts and innovative tactics. The same technology is often available to both sides in a conflict. Yet one side has used that technology effectively and one has not. Why? Winston Churchill provided one answer when he wrote about the early days of World War II: 'I did not comprehend the violence of the revolution effected since the last war by the incursion of a mass of fast-moving armour. I knew about it, but it had not altered my inward convictions as it should have'.[4]

Overcoming the doubts of some of their colleagues, a group of German officers whose inward convictions had been altered became the architects of the successful German *blitzkrieg* assaults of 1939–40. These officers had thought creatively about how to use relatively new technologies and how to integrate them into an overall operational capability. The difference beween the opposing forces, then, was that one side had the force structure, command philosophy, operational concepts and tactics necessary to exploit more fully the capabilities made possible by technology; the other side did not.

Military institutions, like all heavily structured institutions, resist – and at times resent – change, usually with good reasons. The introduction of new technologies on a significant scale demands major upheavals in the training and supply arrangements for the entire force as well as significant alterations in its operational concepts. Moreover, a force can be left vulnerable if the transition to new technology is too rapid or new technologies prove flawed in concept or application – as they sometimes do.

The degree to which technology does and should determine strategy and tactics is always hotly debated. What cannot be disputed, however, is the unbreakable connection between the two and the sterility of analysis that isolates one from the other. Technology should be a tool in the service of strategy. At the same time, that strategy and the implementing operational concepts and tactics should be responsive to the opportunities afforded by technological change.

Bernard Brodie observed about the military commanders prior to World War I that it was their horizons rather than their skill that proved disastrously limited.[5] To ensure that NATO does not repeat that mistake, its military commanders – and political decision-makers – must think creatively. They need to organize their operational concepts into a framework that exploits what new technology has to offer.

Avoid technology as a 'quick and easy answer'. The wide and growing range of technological options imposes difficult choices on defence planners and national policy-makers. What new technology holds out is the promise of making operational skills decisive.[6] Technology contributes to improved conventional performance not only by providing innovative systems that can do things in new ways, but also by enhancing the performance of fielded systems, allowing them to do the same things better.

In a world of rapid transition, high costs and high risks, these possibilities create difficult choices. One choice is between old product improvement and new product acquisition. Some would claim that the latter often degenerates into 'goldplating', making the best the enemy of the good. Despite this criticism, there does exist a legitimate choice about the degree of technological sophistication that is necessary or effective. That choice should be made with a keen recognition of its impact on the speed at which technology can be translated into military hardware and the rate at which hardware can be introduced into the field. It should also be made with a sensitivity to the impact of technological sophistication. Dumb defences can sometimes defeat smart weapons, and there is a limit to what technological sophistication can substitute for the power inherent in numbers.[7]

Another choice exists between the relative emphasis to be placed on (and the allocation of resources to) technology that can be incorporated today versus technology that will have its pay-off in the future. It is the choice between procurement and research and development (R&D), balancing today's threat against tomorrow's. This choice represents the difference between the planner and the commander. The commander's concern is his ability to fight today; the planner's is the ability to fight tomorrow. Both are valid, and it is not always easy to strike the proper balance between them.

A Look to the Future
While one must never forget the relevance of the past when one considers the new, it is equally misleading to ignore the potential uniqueness of the future in stressing the historical continuity of the old. There are several characteristics that seem inherent in much of the new technology that may significantly alter the way NATO needs to think about managing it.

In the past, NATO sought answers about how new technology would affect the military balance (for example, the introduction of battlefield nuclear weapons in the late 1950s or precision-guided munitions in the early 1970s). Today the Alliance seems to have a better understanding of what it wants new technology to do than a knowledge of which systems may be needed to produce the desired result.

New technology will not produce a 'wonder weapon' that is expected to solve all Alliance military shortcomings single-handedly. Rather, current emerging technology encompasses a diffuse range of component technologies which, when netted together and combined with existing weapons, offer the potential to produce a military capability out of all proportion to the increased capability of individual parts.

For example, NATO has long recognized the need for improvement in the amount, availability and accuracy of battlefield information. Such data is necessary to defeat Warsaw Pact operational concepts both by the counter-deployment of NATO's own manoeuvre units and by making its outnumbered fire systems more effective. Here emerging technology offers great promise. Yet, the Alliance is still uncertain about what is the most effective target acquisition sensor technology, what is the most timely and secure method of communicating this information, and how this information is to be processed and shared.

There is a similar degree of uncertainty when one anticipates the use of emerging technology for more effective indirect fire on the enemy: what are the trade-offs in terms of target acquisition, delivery system accuracy, and improvements in the terminal effects of new warheads? If 'smart weapons' have been shown to be inordinately expensive and operationally complex, can 'high IQ' submunitions add increased service life and improved capability to NATO's current inventory of dumb systems?

Uncertainty is both endemic to new technology and indicative of its potential strength. First, the state of the art in the new areas of technology is advancing at an unprecedented rate. For example, the 'weaponization' of microelectronics and composite materials has grown further in the last five years than the technologies of conventional explosives and the internal combustion engine matured over the last fifty. Second, scientific breakthroughs are occurring simultaneously across a broad front of technological application with a high degree of unanticipated overlapping relevance. Third, the component focus of new technologies not only encourages innovation and cross-fertilization, but facilitates its rapid introduction into military systems and their incremental modernization while minimizing costs and block obsolescence.

The very character of the new technology which makes its development so dynamic also challenges NATO's methods of managing it. First, NATO has traditionally focused on new technology in the context of complete weapons systems, the entire design of which was the responsibility of individual governments or a limited consortium. But with new technology the focus will devolve in a direction of nationally-designed and produced components with NATO taking on an increasing role in creating an integrated framework for the netting of subsystems. It will correspondingly have the responsibility of ensuring that the component parts are interoperable.

Second, the component nature of new technology seems to engender, indeed may require, a developmental style of decentralized research, individualized creativity and risk capital. If NATO's technological management approach has been previously dominated by the model of the Manhattan Project and the space programme, perhaps it is time to examine the extraordinary success of the entrepreneurial style associated with the current accelerated advances in information processing. Perhaps it is time to ask whether existing institutional mechanisms inhibit or facilitate the changing nature of technological development.

The third characteristic of the new technology is its changing relationship with the civil sector. In the past, where NATO has focused on major weapons systems (a ship, plane or armoured vehicle), mature technologies associated with these systems have had minimal relationship to civilian R&D. National interests conflicted primarily over who participated in the production of a mass-produced system. However, this is not the case with much of the new technology. With its entrepreneurial emphasis, rapid exploitation of basic research, and component orientation, this technology has a high degree of overlap with the state of the art in non-military applications. If cross-national technology sharing has been difficult in the past, the link between the national competitive edge in global markets and the protection of new technology could make it very difficult indeed. Rather than waging and losing the battle attempting to suppress natural instincts, which may in fact be inducive to healthy competition, it may be important for NATO to explore new management approaches that simultaneously protect emerging technology in the national R&D phase while promoting innovation via competition for the plethora of components which will make up high technology conventional systems of the next decade.

In sum, what appears unique about the nature of emerging technology is the decentralized nature of both its application to the battlefield and its development in the laboratory. If, in fact, the new technology will emerge as a contribution to our collective defence, then NATO's management machinery must be oriented to facilitate this.

On the other hand, given a developmental approach that is oriented towards a component-based emerging technology, this places a premium on existing NATO institutional mechanisms which will be indispensable for providing a mutual, compatible framework for systemic architecture and component integration.

New Technology and Alliance Strengths and Strains

The nature of new technology creates both strengths and strains for the Atlantic Alliance. Those strengths and strains often derive from the same characteristics of that technology.

Operational Concepts

There is no question that new technology can enhance the performance of NATO's conventional forces both by improving the execution of current missions and creating new options. Its impact could be felt across the board. The new operational possibilities created by new technology, however, are also a source of a certain strain within the Alliance. Allies have disagreed about operational applications of new technologies and the relative priority of various roles and missions towards which the new technology should initially be directed.

NATO's experience with the concept of deep attack, an option that new technology is now making available, exemplifies both these strengths and strains. NATO has always considered interdiction an important requirement. What recent deep-attack concepts have attempted to address is how to make this interdiction less risky and more effective.

Deep-attack concepts were designed not to replace forward defence, but to help it succeed. If attacking deep is to make any difference at all, it cannot be pursued in isolation from other developments on the battlefield. It must be closely related to what is happening, for example, on the forward edge of the battle area (FEBA) where first echelons will be engaged.[8]

Those who have criticized deep-attack concepts for being overly offensive have too often confused strategy, operations and tactics. The ideas put forward for deep attack address how specific forces would fight; they are about operations and tactics. There is no inherent contradiction between those ideas and NATO's strategy of forward defence and flexible response. Flexible response can accommodate those ideas and remain a defensive strategy.

On the other hand, while a source of potential strength, it is no secret that there have been considerable differences within NATO over the concept of deep attack. There are several reasons for this. One is a plethora of ideas. Over the last two years the Allies have been exposed to several concepts designed to exploit new technologies – AirLand Battle, Follow-On Forces Attack, Counter Air 90, Army 21 and Emerging Technologies. Quite rightly, the Allies have asked how all of these ideas fit together. A second reason for disagreement has been imprecise language. The 'depth' of a deep attack, for example, was used to mean anything from just beyond direct-fire ranges to distances of hundreds of kilometres. Similarly, it was discovered that West Germany had one definition of the first echelon of Warsaw Pact forces and the US another.

The potential impact of some of the specifics of the deep-attack concept also fostered differences. The question of the delegation of deep-strike authority to lower command levels, for example, created some concern that military operations of such political portent would be insufficiently controlled by political decision-makers. The suggested use of ballistic missiles for runway attack was also criticized because of the possibility that it might lead the opponent to believe that NATO had crossed the nuclear threshold.

Economics

A second set of strengths and strains deriving from the nature of new technology relates to economic considerations. The diffuse nature of the development process of new technology lends itself to the entrepreneurial, free market capitalism of Western economies. The technological base from which NATO can draw is enormous, and it is exploring the entire spectrum of new technologies that could ultimately have an impact on the battlefield. While the United States has 'Silicon Valley', Scotland finds itself the home of 'Silicon Glen', and there is the potential for many other such enterprises throughout Europe. Development of new technology seems to thrive on the 'skunk works' approach characteristic of dynamic, capitalist economies. It is much more difficult for the highly-directed, highly-centralized 'design bureau' approach of the Soviet Union.

A strain emerges, however, when the competition inherent in the Western economic system generates protectionist pressure. Jobs are of greatest concern to most policymakers in the Alliance, and everyone is keenly aware of the economic and political pressures in Europe's high-technology industries. In several areas Europe lags behind the United States and Japan, sometimes severely. Some Europeans are afraid that the United States is trying to consign Europe to the technological poorhouse. Even if it is only to close that gap, there are those who see no choice for Europe but to protect its technological development as they believe others are doing.

Enthusiasm has also been difficult to generate because of the high costs of new technology in the face of lagging economic recovery. It is always possible to demonstrate that new or improved weapons systems incorporating that technology can be beneficial. It is not always possible to convince people that those benefits are worth the costs. How can NATO manage to introduce new technology in a way that is *affordable*?

Decentralization

A third set of strengths and strains flows from the decentralized, component-oriented nature of new technology. As argued earlier, new weapons systems will increasingly represent the integration of a growing number of sub-systems or components, many of which could come from different countries. Given that there are many pieces on which companies can concentrate, numerous opportunities abound for smaller, creative firms. It is not likely that such firms will be predisposed towards sharing development secrets, yet there can be a significant growth in component sharing. Such sharing would strengthen Alliance efforts to promote defence industrial co-operation.

With a greater number of firms engaged in increased sharing, however, technology is more difficult to protect. The fact that there is such considerable civilian-military overlap in the application of new technology also makes it more difficult to keep it from leaking. Not surprisingly, technology leakage has emerged as a strain in Alliance relations.

One problem has been that some technologies that the US has identified as being critical to national security have not been so identified in Alliance capitals. The United States has been criticized for wanting to control too much. Some argued that by taking a comprehensive approach, the Alliance would be less able to protect effectively those technologies that are truly critical to Alliance security. They argued that the real need is first to determine as precisely as possible which goods are militarily relevant, and, second, to identify which strategic goods cannot reasonably be controlled because they are already widely available on international markets.[9]

Other Americans have responded that to match the Soviet Union's full-scale clandestine acquisition effort, the West needs a full-scale prevention effort. Where there is question about whether an item is militarily critical, it is prudent to consider regulating it until it is determined otherwise. At length a new consensus has emerged from the recent and successful COCOM list review on the militarily critical technologies which must be covered by controls.

Another contentious issue is enforcement of the controls that do exist. Here the Americans criticize the Europeans. There is considerable variation among the Allies in their approaches to enforcement and the penalties they impose on violators. In some NATO countries, for example, illegal transfer of technology is not considered a felony. The legal rules should be harmonized, it is argued, even if it requires legislative action. Only then will the Allies be able to reflect a consistent approach to the problem. While differences remain in national approaches, high-level agreement has been reached on the need to improve embargo administration and enforcement. The COCOM subcommittee concerned has recently achieved a number of specific understandings on improvements and harmonization in enforcement.

In the rapidly evolving arena of technology, where the choices are many, the risks and costs high, and the pay-offs potentially enormous, differences over technology are to be expected among allies. Nevertheless, it should be clear that at a time when we all face limited economic horizons combined with soaring R&D costs, the Alliance cannot afford to subsidize the Warsaw Pact's defence industrial base by continuing to leak hard-won technologies to the East. The cost to our economies and to our overall security is simply too great.

The Need for a Resources Strategy
Confronting new problems and faced with new technologies, the temptation is great for NATO to seek new answers, radically different from those of the past. In this author's opinion, radically new solutions for Alliance management of technology are not necessary. NATO does need a new approach, not in the things that it does, but in the way that it does them. It does not need new committees or new instruments, but a new way of putting together the continuing work and maximizing the synergies of processes already established.

If NATO is to manage technology successfully, it must develop what I call a resources strategy.[10] It is a plan of action which integrates and co-ordinates a range of political, military, and economic assets towards the achievement of objectives. The ultimate goal is to get the most out of the limited resources NATO nations devote to defence, and to encourage them to do more, if it is truly necessary.

This 'strategic' approach with regard to resources has become critical in an Alliance with twice the GNP and the same size population as the Warsaw Pact, yet which is out-produced militarily. One can argue that the prime challenge to NATO in its second thirty-five years is the better management of these superior Alliance resources to secure deterrence. If NATO is not funded adequately,

the Alliance ceases to deter. Important action will be impossible and critical objectives unobtainable. A resources strategy, therefore, has two targets: better use of existing resources as a short-term (but continuing) goal; and generation of additional resources for deterrence and defence as a long-term objective. With expensive new technologies, this becomes especially critical. NATO must have a better resources strategy to resolve understandable conflicts of interest and choice, to build on technological strengths, to analyse affordability, to manage timing and change, and to deal with inevitable strains in an Alliance of sixteen sovereign democracies at very different levels of technology with diverse acquisition policies and at different levels of economic recovery.

A successful strategy will capitalize on the very nature of new technology, not run against it. Given the decentralized nature of the development process for new technology, of its impact throughout the spectrum of conventional capabilities and the multiple points of strain and strength, a broad front strategy is required. The elements of a resources strategy should include a better appreciation, a better concept, better planning and co-ordination, better management and co-ordination, better technology protection – and, finally, it requires practical support.

A Better Military Appreciation
A fundamental starting point for the most effective employment of new technology must be a commonly-held appreciation of the military situation that relates the Warsaw Pact threat to NATO's capabilities and puts the change in technology on both sides into proper perspective. 'Bean counts' are a necessary starting point, but one must go beyond them to incorporate the qualitative dimension of the military balance as well. Moreover, there is a need to understand how the situation may be changing. A military appreciation that just takes a snapshot of the current situation and does not present the trends is insufficient for effective policy-making.

NATO today does not prepare a comprehensive and fully-integrated military net assessment that looks at the total balance on each side. The Alliance has suffered as a result, not only from differing perceptions among its members about the threat from the Warsaw Pact but also from lack of agreement about how NATO forces measure up against it.

There is also insufficient common understanding about how technology is affecting the situation. This gives rise to several mistakes. There has been, for example, a tendency to generalize about the overall situation, when the specific situations – between the Central Front and the Southern Flank, for example – are considerably different. Needless to say, the anti-tank balance – and any other technological balance – is not the same for all sectors of the front. There has also been a tendency to equate what NATO has on the drawing boards or in the laboratory with what the Pact has put in the field. The effect has been to skew understanding of how and to what degree Western quality offsets Warsaw Pact quantity.

The Alliance already has many of the elements of a dynamic military appreciation – SACEUR's and SACLANT's annual Combat Effectiveness Report, the military appreciation prepared by the International Military Staff (IMS), and other regular reports. Additional assessments that have been proposed, such as one on the global maritime threat posed by the Soviet Union, present other potential building-blocks.

These studies must be given greater attention by political authorities. Their implications must be better articulated. The findings must be transmitted more effectively back to NATO capitals. These studies must also be more closely co-ordinated and interrelated. Only then will all the Allies have the complete picture, rather than just the pieces of a jigsaw puzzle. They will then be able to locate the appropriately-shaped technology pieces and more clearly understand how technology contributes to the whole.

A Better Conceptual Military Framework
No single doctrinal initiative is a cure-all for NATO. However good, no single improvement – in operating concepts or technology – will provide NATO with a credible conventional deterrent. The challenge is to select the most sensible and practical elements of several approaches and combine them into a coherent effort.

At the December 1983 NATO Defence Ministers meeting, the German Defence Minister, Manfred Wörner, called for the development of a conceptual military framework to integrate the various operational concepts that have been suggested. Picking up Minister Wörner's request, NATO's military authorities have been laying the groundwork for the development of such a framework. The IMS is currently integrating inputs from national capitals and NATO's major military commanders. When it is completed this conceptual military framework should provide a dynamic basis for establishing priorities for NATO's force structure and for providing operational guidelines on how those forces would be used.

Such a framework should clarify much of the confusion that has surrounded the concept of attacking deep by relating it more closely to developments in the forward battle areas where the first echelons are engaged. It should relate military operations to warning indicators and define more precisely the role of tactical intelligence. It should identify how various operational concepts would be tailored to achieve greatest effect in NATO's various geographic sectors where terrain and the local military balance impose different requirements.

An important function of such a conceptual military framework would be to match requirements and technological capabilities. It is here that the lessons learned about the potential for innovative thinking could well be applied.

Better Planning and Co-ordination
NATO does not have a fully co-ordinated process to guide member nations to make decisions in line with Alliance needs. As a consequence there is no agreed basis from which to develop comprehensive priorities, including technological ones.

NATO's force-planning process provides the means by which Alliance planning could be improved. The planning process must also be strengthened by better relating of force planning to that taking place in national capitals. Many of the NATO force goals are heaped on top of national plans. With limited resources devoted to defence, the Allies often cannot pay for the NATO goals. NATO obviously cannot dictate national programmes; but the Alliance can provide better inputs into national planning efforts so that greater harmony among Allied efforts is ensured.

Better planning leads to a better definition of technological needs. Thus it facilitates the decision-making process regarding the difficult technological options confronting NATO policy-makers.

Better Management of NATO's Technological Resources

In addition to these efforts to create a more benign environment for the introduction of new technology, NATO institutions specifically designated to cope with technological change must also be improved.

The major Alliance organization for managing technology is the Conference of National Armaments Directors (CNAD). It was established when the issues became too complex for effective consideration in the old Naval, Air Force and Army Armaments Groups. CNAD was based on each nation's belief that it needed a single national spokesman for the political, economic and technical aspects of armaments research, development and acquisition.

The CNAD organization now consists of nearly 240 groups, panels and special committees, linked through the National Armaments Directors and their resident representatives at NATO Headquarters. There is also a NATO Industrial Advisory Group (NIAG) – 14 national representatives backed by industrialists with the task of advising and assisting the CNAD from the industrial perspective.

Looking back, the CNAD and its ancillary bodies have had significant successes – the F-16 fighter programme, and E3A AWACS (Airborne Warning and Control System) among them. European nations are justly proud of the *Roland* and the *Leopard* II Main Battle Tank. On the horizon are the NATO frigate programme, the NATO helicopter and the Multiple Launch Rocket System (MLRS).

The Emerging Technology (ET) Initiative is a special CNAD effort to deal effectively with the introduction of new technology. The ET Initiative is intended to capitalize on new technology's promise for:

– Better tailoring capabilities to the actual threat, and exploiting Pact vulnerabilities;
– Improving the performance of weapons platforms without making significant and expensive alterations to those platforms or introducing costly new ones;
– Increasing the operational synergism of existing capabilities.

NATO has initially concentrated on trying to exploit newly-available technology. The first step was a series of studies examining the potential impact of those technologies in NATO's various geographic regions. Then, in the Spring of 1984, CNAD agreed on several areas of technology that could usefully be pursued on a co-operative Alliance basis. Those areas were subsequently approved by Defence Ministers. Work is now under way in the various groups under the CNAD umbrella to take those technologies and integrate them into operative military systems. The first step is the resolution of differences over military requirements and the delineation of specific co-operative ventures.

Two further points should be made about the ET Initiative. First, it has been an integrative effort, spurring political, military and industrial managers to work together. They have had to admit to areas of common interest that have traditionally been considered in isolation. Second, the ET effort is not a 'buy America' programme. Rather, it aims to improve the military capabilities of the Alliance in a way that is responsive to the economic and political imperatives of each Alliance member.

The list of opportunities seems endless, but success should not be assumed. Several steps should be taken to move the process of managing Alliance technology forward. One is to strengthen the Independent European Programme Group (IEPG). This group, which includes France, was formed to rationalize the European defence sector and enable it to take part in arms co-operation with the US on a more equal footing. Bolstering the IEPG will allow it to represent more effectively the 'European' perspective on critical technology measures within CNAD. This is now being done under the very able leadership of its Dutch chairman, State Minister van Houwelingen.

Better use can be made of the CNAD representatives in Brussels. The links to industry can be strengthened and the transmission belt from the NIAG to CNAD made more effective. Closer co-operation should also be fostered between military planners and military technologists both at NATO and in national capitals.

The process must also be strengthened above the CNAD level. Policy-makers, not just experts, must devote greater time and attention to technology issues. Those issues should be thoroughly examined by both the Defence and Foreign Minister. More senior levels of the decision-making process at NATO Headquarters, such as the Executive Working Group, must also be brought more into the process.

Improved Armaments Co-operation
Transatlantic arms trade will be an important mechanism for sharing technology throughout the Alliance. Therefore, improved armaments co-operation is a critical component of a resources strategy.

There has been a chorus of complaint in Europe about the unequal traffic on the transatlantic two-way street. The aggregate balance favours the United States by between three to one and seven to one depending on the figures used. It is naïve to believe, however, that the bilateral defence trade of European NATO members with the United States will magically be brought into even a rough balance. The differences in industrial base, markets and other factors are just too great. R&D investment by the United States, for example, is seven times higher than for all her European Allies combined. Nevertheless, a better balance in the transatlantic arms trade must be achieved. Co-operative efforts must be strengthened on both the industrial and the government levels.

Transatlantic armaments co-operation is US policy, and it is NATO policy. But better mechanisms are needed to implement that policy. In the United States, the executive and legislative branches of government must develop an agreement and an action plan in concert with private industry and labour. That process has already begun with both the Department of Defense and the Department of State giving greater attention to armaments co-operation issues. Congress has demonstrated its willingness to play a helpful role with the passage of the Glenn–Roth–Nunn Amendment supporting better arms co-operation by a vote of 87 to 1. Industry has made it clear that it will embrace greater arms co-operation if it is a US government priority.

Europe must also get its house in order. It must increase its investment in R&D and, in fact, the idea of a European Advanced Research Agency has already been floated by the North Atlantic Assembly.[11] European members of the Alliance must also organize their industrial structures and their markets on scale more competitive with those of the United States. An important element in this effort will be the work of the IEPG. If other forces are also successful at promoting greater European co-operation, the United States would welcome that development as long as it is complementary and not competitive with NATO efforts.

Co-operation is not easy. It must overcome tough issues such as offsets, work sharing, third-country sales and competition. Perhaps the most dangerous problem is the growth of technological protectionism. In the long run, a resurgence of protectionism could prove as damaging to the Alliance as neglecting its conventional forces.

No single NATO nation can do the job alone. Just as NATO's approach to operational concepts must be innovative, so creative approaches that make the most of the explosion in technological development can make the West's industrial diversity a major contributor to the common defence.

Technology Protection
Greater sharing of technology must go hand in hand with greater technology protection. It is part of the job of a resources strategy to implement this harmonization. On the one hand, we cannot allow vital technology to aid a Soviet military build-up that in turn forces NATO to take expensive counter-measures.

On the other, good strategy will also promote the rate at which the West incorporates its technology into Alliance weapons systems.

Progress in resolving differences on the protection of critical technologies. The recent agreement in COCOM to update controls on computers and to regulate software exports is an important step. The initiation of a 'Red Side' analysis which looks at the advantages to the Warsaw Pact of the flow of technology is another.

The Alliance must build on these steps in a way that maximizes progress on a multilateral front. Piecemeal, bilateral efforts between Alliance nations could prove so complex as to be ultimately unworkable. An argument can be made, for example, that NATO should have a larger management role in the protection of technology. NATO can contribute a well-developed structure and process for the settlement of disputes as well as a rich military and political context within which to assess the impact of specific technologies.

Unfortunately there has been considerable reluctance to discuss technology protection within NATO councils. COCOM is still considered in many capitals to be the only proper forum for such discussions. COCOM is taking steps better to meet the challenge – strengthening its procedures to identify, track and control militarily significant technology. However, COCOM does not concern itself directly with non-trade aspects of technology protection. A way must also be found to capitalize on the benefits that the NATO process has to offer since greater technology sharing in the Alliance will ultimately be dependent on parallel progress in technology protection.

Political Support
The final element in an effective NATO resources strategy is the political consensus that bonds the military and economic factors together. However sound Alliance military strategy, however well-conceived its arms procurement, however sophisticated its technology, only political consensus and enlightened, resolute Alliance leadership can realize the benefits of new technology for strengthened conventional deterrence.

NATO is not a supranational organization, able to impose measures on member nations. They will only grudgingly give up the prerogatives of their sovereignty, and will most often give precedence to national programmes. While great progress might be made at NATO Headquarters, impediments in NATO capitals can bring to an abrupt halt any momentum that might be generated in Brussels.

Coalitions must be built, and that process must start in Alliance capitals. It must occur not just in Defence and Foreign Ministries but in Finance Ministries and Trade and Industry Ministries as well. It must also extend to national legislatures.

Links between NATO Headquarters and national capitals must be strengthened. Politicians need a proper appreciation and a conceptual military framework as badly as the military authorities, and it is not uncommon for policy-makers in capitals to be unaware of all that is happening at NATO Headquarters and *vice versa*. During the difficult days prior to the initial deployment of *Pershing* II and cruise missiles last autumn, the links between Brussels and the national capitals were exceptionally strong, largely as the result of the work of the Special Consultative Group and the High Level Group. Building on this admirable example, NATO should find a way to improve the transmission belts between Alliance Headquarters and capitals on the whole range of issues associated with improving conventional defence, including the technological choices that are now being made or that must be made in the future.

Conclusion
New technology can be a source of great strength to the Alliance. At its most basic it can improve the military performance of NATO's armed forces. In so doing, technology could make a considerable contribution to enhancing deterrence. Economic spin-offs could be generated, adding to the economic rejuvenation of all Alliance members. Political harmony could be fostered deriving from the co-operation that will be absolutely essential if the process is to be successful.

Technology is a tool, and like any tool it can be helpful only if we know what to do with it and then choose to use it. That knowledge is often hard to come by, and that choice is not often easy. But in the NATO context the needs of deterrence and defence are well defined. The issue is whether the Alliance will be able to manage its resources, including technology, to meet those needs. Ultimately, the issue will be decided by the vision and leadership in NATO capitals and in Brussels.

NOTES

[1] Thomas A. Callaghan, Jr, 'The Structural Disarmament of NATO,' *NATO Review*, June 1984, no. 3.

[2] 'How Far Should US go to Regulate its Technology Exports?' *Christian Science Monitor*, 16 May 1984 and 'Keeping Technology out of Soviet Hands Appears Impossible', *Wall Street Journal*, 15 August 1984.

[3] For a discussion of this point relative to the Falklands War and the Israeli invasion of Lebanon, see Michael Moodie, 'Six Months, Three Wars', *The Washington Quarterly*, Autumn 1982.

[4] Quoted in John J. Mearsheimer, Conventional Deterrence (Ithaca, NY: Cornell UP, 1983), p. 97.

[5] Bernard Brodie, 'Strategy in the Missile Age' (Princeton, NJ: Princeton UP, 1959), p. 59.

[6] Michael Howard, 'The Forgotten Dimensions of Strategy', *Foreign Affairs*, Summer 1979.

[7] Joseph Joffe, 'Is NATO Building an Achilles Heel?' *Wall Street Journal*, 13 June 1984.

[8] For greater elaboration of this point, see Philip A. Karber, 'In Defense of Forward Defense', *Armed Forces International*, May 1984, p. 46.

[9] See, for example, the speech by Mr Norman Tebbitt, Britain's Minister for Trade and Industry, to the North American section of London's Chamber of Commerce, cited in *Science*, 11 May 1984, p. 579.

[10] While the views presented in this Paper are those of the author and address issues on which in some cases NATO and the government of the United States have not as yet taken positions, the need for a 'resources strategy, enlarged here but first articulated in a speech to the Atlantic Treaty Association in November 1983 has since been recognized in the DPC communiqué of May 1984 and is being addressed by NATO's Executive Working Group.

[11] 'Europe Seeks a NATO Research Agency', *Aviation Week and Space Technology*, 4 June 1984.

Defence Research and Development and Western Industrial Policy: Part I

PROF. SIR RONALD MASON

The support of research and development (R&D) in science and technology – its extent, structure, rationale and the way in which criteria for support vary from country to country – are matters of great interest to any student of scientific, industrial and societal policies. In the US, USSR and Western Europe, defence R&D is of especial import in view of the resources allocated and their effect on other possible priorities.

There is a sharp need to distinguish R&D and, even under the research head, the expectations attached to research activities – whether the objectives are 'pure and disinterested', 'strategic' or 'applied'. In the four major industrial countries of the West, little or no defence research has anything but strategic or applied aims; innovative activity is directed to a realization of strategic objectives – perhaps for a quick, far-sighted broadly-based requirement necessitating rather longer term programmes than would be envisaged for applied research. For the latter, one may assume that the main 'barrier' questions have been answered. The science, technology and engineering needed to implement, say, directed-energy weapons in space must be regarded as strategic research, as must important areas of 'stealth' systems; that which is needed to produce cost-effective solutions to the requirement of conventional deep strike against mobile targets must be regarded similarly; that which is needed, say, to further improve the CEP of ballistic missile re-entry bodies borders on straightforward development.

Having said that, however, one recognizes grey areas and the lack of really clear distinctions so that defence R&D policies and their management have far from clear and objective guidelines. They are, quite often, dictated by extrinsic (politico-industrial) factors rather than intrinsic parameters. But it is the case also that the defence budgets of the US, Britain, France and the FRG all bear very similar R&D costs, as proportions of total budgets; three years ago the R&D vote for all of these countries was 14 ± 2% of the respective defence budgets (the Soviet Union was around 21–22%). British spending on *research* was the lowest proportionately – in 1980–81, this amounted to 4% of procurement or about 2% of the defence budget while development accounted for 26% of procurement or 12% of the defence budget (some 42% of the defence budget was spent on equipment, some 20% more than four years earlier and a trend which is now reflected in increasingly well-equipped defence forces).

These bare statistical data deserve two comments which, although relating to Britain in particular, do have some general value. The first is that over one-half of British government R&D funds go to defence (and by some arguments that is too high a proportion of national resources). But the majority of these funds go to development by and in industry. There has been a clear policy decision to maintain a broad-based defence industry to support defence policies which have wider responsibilities and requirements than any other country with a comparable economy. Typically, the equipment budget provides 40% for aircraft and associated equipment/weapons, 30% to ships and maritime equipment and weapons and a little more than 20% to land systems and vehicles (a little less than 10% is dedicated to general support). It is, quite simply, a major change of defence policy – reducing, say, one of our major commitments to NATO – which is necessary to bring defence R&D funds down to a level, measured as a proportion of GNP,

15

to those of France and the FRG. Secondly, Britain has, over nearly a decade, maintained a ratio of R&D expenditures to production expenditure of 1:2.2. By most commercial standards this is a relatively unfavourable ratio but we see here some reflection of the sophistication of defence equipment which in turn is inexorably dictated by the nature of the threat. It could be improved towards, say, the FRG R&D/production ratio by at least three devices: by more off-shore purchases (80% of British equipment expenditure goes on national contracts placed with British industry and 15% to the British share of collaborative projects); by increasing participation in collaborative development programmes and other forms of co-operation; and by seeking greater commonality with civil high-technology programmes and products. These are matters which are looked at in more detail in this Paper.

It follows that the construction of defence R&D policy must be set in the context of defence policy itself and the related operational requirements and in the context of technology and engineering opportunities and their implications for incremental or major changes in investment in different weapon systems. Finally it must be based on judgments of national industrial capabilities, existent or planned.

What might be called the interaction of operational requirements with developments in technologies and weapon systems forms the essential base of a defence research and, more to the point, an advanced development programme. The requirements and the systems' possibilities may not often be in phase and it is often suggested that 'doctrine must lead and technical feasibility follow'. That ignores the real but very subtle synergistic relations between national and international policies, between those programmes which have socio-economic benefits and the often totally independent discoveries in science and their implementation in new technologies. We are certainly at the point where the dynamic of technological change is greater than that which can be associated with politico-social processes; technology is certainly not everything but increasingly it creates opportunities and vulnerabilities

which are reacted to rather than planned for in political or social processes. There is certainty in Japan and the United States that 'high technology' must form the base of further economic development; there is increasing agreement in Western Europe also on this strategy although a consensus is under pressure from time to time for a variety of reasons, mostly announced by political fringe groups. The real requirements which an R&D programme must meet for the foreseeable future (assuming that manpower and budgets may at best remain at present levels) are that we will continue to rely on an equipment-manpower mix which is oriented towards equipment; that technology must increasingly be a force multiplier; that we must achieve force multiplication of a number of defence capabilities through the technical improvement of the system or systems contributing to a capability; and associated doctrinal adjustments.

There has been general agreement in NATO on the particular areas of technology which are of increasing importance in the development of conventional forces. They are for the most part related to electronics and materials. The primary and important capabilities to be enhanced are: weapon guidance and control; command, control and information systems; and electronic warfare and related areas relying on advances in electronics technology and devices. There would seem to be general agreement that only secondary advances can be foreseen in platform performance and then only in rather special equipments, such as V/STOL (Vertical/Short Take-Off and Landing) or STOVL (Short Take-Off and Vertical Landing) aircraft and particularly long-endurance aircraft for surveillance and reconnaissance.

These 'emergent technologies' are, of course, forming part of the major debate in the Alliance which, in broad terms, is concerned with raising the nuclear threshold through a significant upgrading of conventional defence and deterrence capabilities. The particular strategic technologies, a number of which are already in place, are those which overlap onto civil programmes in the US, Japan and Western Europe: microelectronics with emphasis on very high speed integrated circuits (VHSIC); advanced software and high speed algorithm development and machine intelligence; active and passive electronic warfare including signature reduction ('stealth'); new composite materials and advanced warhead designs and materials; particular electronic devices such as high density focal plane arrays; and optoelectronics (lasers).

The uncertainties in a future R&D programme centred around these do not lie with the technologies *per se*; rather it is in the development of the total (weapon) systems with particular characteristics and properties and hence meeting certain operational requirements. The equation of 'emerging technologies' with enhanced capabilities is simplistic, if literally interpreted. System complexity, integration and reliability is being greatly improved by computer-aided design and manufacture; and by the impact of advanced manufacturing technology on batch production processes. But it is here that the prospects for collaboration on equipment begin to look difficult.

There is considerable symmetry between the technical and industrial capabilities of Western Europe and the United States. There are obvious differences of scale but, despite assertions that have come from the United States, the technology gap is not large. There are gaps in systems engineering and in systems implementation which originate in part in the fragmentary national efforts which mark systems development in Western Europe (parenthetically one notes the success of Japan at the total systems approach with the introduction of very successful systems often based on 'yesterday's technology' rather than having a high technical sophistication of components).

Political and economic arguments obviously preclude a future in which the United States uniquely exploits the developments with the rest of the Alliance simply procuring products. The 'two way street' is likely to become more unbalanced unless there is an agreed joint development of weapon systems whose priorities have been recognized by the publication of Memoranda of Understanding (MOU) or staff targets. Industries could then pick up requirements and seek case-by-case arrangements with industries in other countries on a commercial basis. Difficult problems, such as intellectual property rights, can be tackled in a pragmatic way as the development proceeds. Mechanisms such as those used by the infrastructure group for the procurement of air defence radar systems could surely be extended to weapon systems.

The opportunities are present: collaboration should reflect on technical and industrial complementarities and the choice of weapon system(s) on their relative force multiplication value. Thus we understand in Europe, and with little dissent from the United States, that the requirements of surveillance C³ (communications, command and control) should be amongst the first for enhancement – an agreed set of solutions would have a major impact and would capitalize on the standing of (civil) information technology in the West. Secondly, we have the counter-air requirement – largely through the denial of airfield use. There is little disagreement that long-range (up to 300 km) interdiction against high-value static assets is best achieved using penetrating stand-off weapon systems – which one might speculate to be second generation air-launched cruise missiles (ALCM). Thirdly, the relatively short-range (up to about 30 km beyond the FEBA) anti-armour capability needs to be – and can be – rapidly enhanced using directed munitions or submunitions with relatively straightforward guidance and data processing capabilities available *now*. Lastly, there is a vital need for the Alliance to react coherently to the chemical threat and it needs to be noted that chemical defence technologies are at their most developed in Europe.

Significant opportunities also exist for collaboration on maritime-air weapon systems, but that need not be rehearsed here. The essential point to set down is a simple one: unless there is early agreement on requirements, development policies, and industrial collaboration, Alliance members will be forced into (national) role specialization – and that specialization will be difficult to separate from isolationism. The political challenge is to see that Alliance defence is synonymous with Western security, and that properly constructed R&D programmes can themselves act as deterrents as well as providing the basis for defence capabilities into the next century. But the political parochialisms and industrial suspicions which have marked the past must give way to collaboration based on enlightened self-interest where the overall objective is to further stabilize the West and release resources for meeting the inevitable challenges, the inevitable call for different dependencies and interdependencies, which will emerge in Asia and Africa.

Defence Research and Development and Western Industrial Policy: Part II

HENRI MARTRE

The prime objective of R&D in the area of defence is to ensure the capability of the armed forces for the years ahead. It is characterized both by its extreme importance and the considerable problems inherent in it.

Its importance stems from the fact that its aim is to ensure the continuity of a nation's security, and any error in this field can therefore influence the outcome of a battle, or even a war, and thus affect the destiny of an entire people. The history books are full of examples where qualitative weapons superiority or, even more important, the surprise created by the appearance of new weapons have proved decisive in determining the outcome of a conflict. In this respect one need only mention such innovations as artillery, radar and nuclear weapons. Also of considerable importance is the extent of the financial outlay generated by a military hardware renewal and modernization policy, since this outlay comprises not only the intrinsic cost of R&D, which accounts for 25–30% of the weapons budget for a country producing its own equipment, but also the cost of replacing equipment which, although not at the end of its active life, is considered to be obsolete, plus the cost of training and logistics necessitated by the introduction of this new equipment into the armed forces.

The definition and implementation of such an R&D policy also gives rise to considerable problems, chiefly because of the time needed for these innovations to mature and because of the technical and political changes which can occur in the meanwhile. Indeed, ten to twenty years may be needed from the discovery of a physical phenomenon until its potential military application is fully demonstrated. Similarly, another ten or so years may elapse between the launching of a research programme and the introduction of the relevant equipment into the armed forces. It is thus obvious that it is far from easy to foresee, so far in advance, what will be the actual operational impact of a discovery and even harder to imagine its interaction with other discoveries yet to be made, some of which might supersede it completely and some of which might negate its effects.

Those in charge of directing a defence R&D policy, defining the objectives and making the consequent choices, thus have to bear a burden of responsibility made all the heavier by the weight of uncertainty attached to it. They can afford to neglect nothing which later (too late) could prove to be of major interest. They must nevertheless be thrifty since the resources made available to them will be fiercely disputed by those responsible for the maintenance of existing equipment and the operational readiness of the forces. Efficiency and balance are thus the two main guidelines of their choices. *Efficiency*, since the resources must be reserved for those innovations capable of providing the greatest military benefit in relation to their cost and the best working teams and laboratories. *Balance* must be achieved in various ways. First, to take account of the chronological intermeshing of the various projects. Each has a deadline and they must all be combined in such a way that at all times in the future, both short- and long-term, the military requirements are met. Then, balance must be achieved between the various operational functions to be performed in the context of a given military policy. It is clear that the armed forces can only carry out their missions if they are able to perform a certain number of complementary functions: they must control the situation by means of intelligence and communications, be ready to attack at various ranges, to protect themselves, etc. Finally, one must not lose sight of the fact that for given research activities, changes in military policy could quite possibly occur, thus creating new needs.

Nationalism and Alliance

These are only general principles and each country is obliged to adapt its policies and its projects to meet its financial capacity and scientific, technical and industrial resources. This much is obvious, but it must also adapt them to the rate at which military technology is progressing. This rate is essentially imposed by the competition between the Warsaw Pact countries and those of NATO and by the vast extent of the resources devoted to defence by the two super-powers. This competition is indeed at the root of the main advances made in the weapons field over the last thirty years. Some of these were brought about by derivations and innovations in the civilian sector but which themselves occurred within the framework of this competition. The major Alliances do not, however, hold a monopoly on arms. Other countries are active in this field but, for their products to have any military value and operational competitiveness, they must be brought into line with the characteristics of those created by the major powers. However, the disproportion of financial and technical means obliges those countries who wish to follow a relatively independent arms policy to adopt specific approaches and choose a limited number of market openings of a complexity suited to their capabilities. Experience has shown that this is possible and that, despite the differences in their sizes, many developed (and even developing) nations are setting up arms industries and creating new products.

This phenomenon exists even within NATO itself. For reasons of political equilibrium, but also for industrial and economic reasons, the Allies do not wish to allow the United States a monopoly on arms production, or even development, and they participate in these activities in proportion to the resources they devote to defence. The leading European members of NATO even hope to be essentially self-sufficient in military equipment, by virtue of their own industrial capacity, and they have to a large extent succeeded. How have they managed to do this, when the United States has a military R&D budget five to ten times greater than that of each of the main Western European countries? The reasons are many. The first is that these countries do not develop a product range as wide as that of the United States. Only two of them, Britain and France, produce nuclear weapons and even these two countries, whose product catalogues are the most complete, are not involved in a certain number of programmes. The second reason is that the European countries have appreciably lower development costs than the United States. This is quite simply due to the fact that, having less resources available, they must adopt different methods. In particular, they explore fewer hypothetical avenues, carry out less parallel work and their test programmes have a lower level of redundancy. Similarly, disposing (as they do) fewer work teams, laboratories and industrial plants, government relations with them are less rigid and more continuous. The third reason is that the European countries have benefited from technological transfers from the United States. These transfers have occurred through the granting of licences for the production of certain equipment or components. They have also received information, which, whilst not constituting a technology transfer, has enabled them to orient their work, using public literature or in the context of data exchange agreements. The fourth reason is that the European countries have to a considerable extent co-operated, allowing them to share programme development costs. This has been particularly the case in many aircraft and missile programmes, which are among the most costly. Finally, one must not forget to mention that a certain number of them broadened their military industrial base by exporting equipment within the framework of their foreign policy, and this broadening has enabled them to amortize at least part of their fixed costs.

The combination of these factors has allowed Western Europe to develop and produce the majority of the weapons needed for its defence, weapons of a technical and operational sophistication which are equivalent to the equipment produced by the United States.

Rationalization, Standardization and Interoperability

The question has often been asked whether there is duplication in this area, and therefore wasteful use of resources which is in the long-run prejudicial to the common defence effort. It cannot be denied that, were the United States to produce all the arms for the Alliance, they would be created and produced in better economic conditions thanks to a greater level of amortization of the fixed costs and to the large scale of the production runs. The idea of this degree of concentration is, however, purely hypothetical and comes up against major political and economic objections. The first of these is that the Alliance is formed to combat a common threat, but this does not imply alignment of the foreign and military policies of the Allied countries. These countries retain their independence and responsibility for the defence of their own interests which go much further than the objectives of the Alliance. Their capacity for independent decision-making remains. Another objection is that arms expenditure ties up a substantial part of national resources and no industrialized nation can agree to export this in full, for it would deprive its own economy and industries, in particular at a time when the problems of unemployment are being keenly felt. From a more military point of view, it is quite possible that extensive standardization of arms would entail more problems than gains. The threats are indeed very varied, whether in regard to the weapons of the adversary, the terrain or the circumstances, and the way that they might be used. One must therefore have widely diversified equipment if one is to be in a position to face all possible situations. This is all the more true given the increasing complexity of weapons systems and the development of counter-measures of all descriptions. It is clear that total standardization would make the enemy's task that much easier, enabling him to develop a limited number of defences and counter-measures, whereas diversification obliges him to spread his efforts. This principle is widely applied by the US in her own arms programmes. For a given military mission, the US often simultaneously commissions several weapons systems with characteristics as different as possible. Similarly, from an industrial point of view, she practices a policy of competition between the various arms manufacturers rather than one of rationalization, precisely in order to benefit from the best ideas available. In these conditions, it would be wrong to emasculate the European industrial potential when it is in a position to make a substantial contribution to the defence of the continent.

Diversity must not, however, be confused with dispersal and the abandonment of all attempts at rationalization of the Alliance's resources. On the contrary, it is essential that the armed forces of the Allied countries be capable of operating together under the most effective conditions. This brings up the problem of interoperability, a problem which has been widely examined and one which is of particular importance with regard to telecommunications, ammunition and fuels. Interoperability can however extend to many other important areas of logistic support, including major supply items, methods of transport, etc. Similarly, precautions must be taken and considerable attention must be paid to concentrating all efforts on significant projects and avoiding a pointless and wasteful overlapping and duplication of effort.

Industrial Policy

The problem arises to what extent the development of technologies and weapons will influence the way in which the programmes are implemented and indeed the whole industrial policy of the NATO countries. Much is heard of the new 'emerging technologies' and the important changes to military policy which they could bring about and it could be beneficial to examine their possible industrial impact. One should note first that technological progress was particularly rapid during and after World War II and that the industrial structures then underwent a permanent transformation without any real discontinuity. There is therefore no reason to believe that the present changes will create a rupture and trigger an industrial revolution.

However, among the factors which could accelerate the movement, the two most significant should be underlined. The first is that the complexity of weapons systems would appear to be increasing at a faster rate than in the past, and that the development and acquisition costs are also rising. The second is that the gravity of the international situation following the second oil crisis interrupted the economic growth of the NATO countries and their budgetary resources, and they are now therefore less able to meet an increase in the cost of their military equipment than in the past. A certain number of analysts have shown that the unit cost of arms in constant money terms in the long-term rose once at the same rate as the cost of living in the industrial nations. These nations thus believed that they could bear the cost of the progressive increase in sophistication of their equipment without too much trouble. This is now no longer the case and is a fundamental reason for paying even greater attention to the economy of weapons programmes.

One must first examine the unavoidable nature of the increasing complexity of weapons systems, in particular for the future. All technologies can be seen to be advancing at various rates but the fields in which the most significant progress is being made are electronics and information technologies. The digitalizing of data and the miniaturization of circuits are opening an increasing number of doors to the designer and user, and processing capacity has been multiplied many times in only a few years. This multiplication of the number of computation functions available endows the systems with a much wider performance range, extends their operating modes and protects them from enemy counter-measures, whilst at the same time facilitating and simplifying the task of the operator. These are therefore advantages which can only be neglected at the risk of finding oneself irreversibly outclassed in combat. The same applies to less spectacular innovations but which are still of great military interest, including increasing weapons accuracy and range. One must, however, be wary of falling into excess, and a clear line must be drawn between real operational advantages and those developments which present only a marginal benefit.

Complexity and Cost

If the growth of equipment complexity and costs cannot be avoided, and if the resources available fail to keep pace with this growth, how can one escape marked reduction in the capabilities of the armed forces? Two avenues have already been explored and are worth further investigation. The first consists in pooling resources to develop new equipment. The second aims at optimizing the use of resources by means of closer association between administration and industry.

For the last twenty years, the European NATO countries have co-operated on a fairly wide basis and with a fair measure of success. This meant that development costs were shared by the partners although the overall cost was slightly higher due to the very nature of the co-operation process. Nations have had to compromise on specifications and there has been a certain unwieldiness in the running of the programmes. Co-operation did not, however, permit significant economies to be achieved in production costs because of the need to break up and share the industrial workloads, even if it was possible to organize single-source production of most components. The main, and extremely important, advantage of this process was to bring the European companies to work together, to broaden their mutual understanding and to create efficient organizations.

One can now safely say that the groundwork for increased European co-operation has been successfully laid and it is clear that the awareness of the need for this co-operation is increasingly present in the minds of those concerned. Numerous preliminary consultations between the various countries have thus been held at both governmental and industrial levels to discuss the launching of important new programmes. This spirit of co-operation, which was already common for the major countries, now extends to others and joint projects involving four or five countries are appearing. This development can only be applauded, since it is consistent with the current need to adapt to a changing situation. One must not, however, lose sight of its limitations.

The first of these stems from the fact that sharing development costs results in a significant, although far from massive, saving in the programme cost. Statistics relating to a few operations involving diverse technologies show that a saving of only about 10% of the total cost of the programme can be achieved through co-operation. Another limitation, rather more difficult to evaluate with any accuracy, is that caused by the increase in the number of partners. There is a long history of co-operation between two and sometimes even three partners, but there is some uncertainty as to the efficiency of co-operation involving more numerous associations. Some are highly sceptical on this matter and very pessimistic views have been put forward. One can however hope that realism and the spirit of compromise will prevail over the forces of division.

Other suggestions have been that, in order to make co-operation more profitable, a much closer association between the industrial partners is necessary, even going as far as merging them. Alternatively, the various European countries should specialize and divide up the arms industry between themselves, each country dealing with a particular field of activity on behalf of all the others. These ideas are interesting, but are likely to remain just ideas for as long as the political organization of Europe remains as it is today. It is indeed hard to imagine independent governments, albeit allied and co-operating in many fields, permanently surrendering the independence of their industrial power which is a prerogative of their national sovereignty.

Co-operation in Arms Procurement

The problem of developing co-operation between Europe and the United States also arises when one looks at how to strengthen the effectiveness of the Alliance. One is obliged to recognize, however, that the context is very different from that which has just been examined. The scale is much greater than for the other countries in the Alliance taken individually and the United States' remoteness from the European theatre means that her own ambitions and strategic preoccupations are not easily integrated into a framework of co-operation. In addition, the US Administration does not favour long-term

financial commitments implied by the launching of an international programme and it applies a set of rules which, designed for internal use, are ill-adapted to the complex nature of joint work based on compromise and flexibility. This means that, despite the scope of the American programmes, very few of them are carried out on a basis of true co-operation. This does not mean, however, that this number cannot be increased, but it does mean that it will be a long, hard road and results cannot be expected in the medium term.

Relations between the United States and Europe in the armaments field are nevertheless many and varied and their effectiveness should not be underestimated. At an official level, there is a large-scale exchange of scientific and technical data allowing optimum orientation of programmes and thus avoiding needless and wasteful expenditure of energy. Furthermore, the European countries which cannot develop all the types of equipment they need turn to the United States, either for direct purchases, or for manufacture under licence. It must be admitted that the Americans are aware of the economic problems of their partners and do their best to find ways of compensating on an industrial basis. This is not really the 'two-way street' we had imagined, but the tendency is in this direction and there is hope that the balance of exchanges with Europe will be less unbalanced in the future.

Finally, the industrial relations between both sides of the Atlantic are particularly well-developed and their flexibility imparts a high level of efficiency. There is little doubt that it is towards extending these relations that the most effort should be devoted, since they constitute a basis for later concrete co-operation. This presupposes, however, that the obstacles be not too great and that the US Administration continue a relevant open policy of technological transfer with its allies.

Free Competition versus Rationalization

It remains to be determined to what extent industry can be made more cost-effective, both in design and production. This is a large subject for discussion which tends to oppose the advocates of total competition and those of excessive rationalization. There is no doubt that competition does stimulate the imagination and provide a strong incentive to reduce costs. It must not, however, be forgotten that arms production involves the incorporation of very high technology over relatively long periods of time and entails considerable intellectual investment and costly equipment which rapidly becomes obsolete. In this field, dynamism is essential, but success can only be obtained through an accumulation of skills and experience maintained only by the strictest continuity. Continuity of this kind is incompatible with the contingencies of competition which involves constant adaptation to meet the changing situation. The acceptable ground therefore lies somewhere between the two and it is the responsibility of the governments to combine stimulation with continuity, a task which is clearly far from easy.

With continuity in mind, it is important to avoid sudden changes of direction in the running of programmes, such as could result from variations in the technical orientation or from financial difficulties. This implies that the programme launch decisions must be very carefully weighed in advance.

As a general rule, the economic running of a programme can only be successful if pragmatic and permanent account is taken of all elements of industrial management, in the same way as economic running of a car demands that the characteristics of the engine be taken into account. This can only be done if there is close co-operation between governmental departments and industry, and provided there is mutual understanding of the difficulties experienced by each.

There would therefore seem to be no miracle cure for the problem of the increasing complexity and cost of arms equipment arising from the constantly accelerating technical advances being made, advances with which the resources available cannot keep pace. Only a pragmatic approach to the questions of international co-operation and industrial politics will allow present trends to be improved and this demands from all those concerned, both government and industry, understanding, a spirit of compromise and a firm will to succeed.

The 'Star Wars' Debate: The Western Alliance and Strategic Defence: Part I

Twelve years after the Anti-Ballistic Missile (ABM) Treaty emerged from SALT I and seemed to drive a stake through the heart of proposals to build a Ballistic Missile Defence (BMD), they are once more in our midst as an element of the strategic debate. President Reagan's speech of 23 March 1983 revived the issue. What has come to be known as his Strategic Defense Initiative (SDI) has been a major theme of strategic discourse in Western countries since then.

A reconsideration of the basis for the earlier US decision to abandon active defences is an appropriate starting point for evaluating the SDI. The doctrine of Mutual Assured Destruction (MAD) supplied the rationale for that decision and was in turn apotheosized by the ABM Treaty. The assumptions underlying MAD prejudged the key question of how effective defences had to be to be useful. When assessed in a more realistic framework than MAD, defences do not have to be nearly leakproof to be useful in deterring Soviet attack.

Technological advances have also radically changed the outlook on how effective ballistic missile defences can be. 'Emerging technologies' offer the possibility of a BMD that is quite different in important respects from those that were considered and rejected earlier. The new opportunities for BMD may have quite different implications for the long-term future of the arms competition with the Soviet Union from those projected by opponents during the earlier debate. Of special interest to major allies of the US is the prospect of a robust defence against theatre ballistic missiles. In fact this could well turn out to be the earliest application of the SDI technologies.

Much of the comment on the SDI seems to be directed towards a proposal to begin imme-diately the deployment of BMD. But no such issue is before us; the President's speech dealt instead with the goal of a long-term R&D programme and its implications for Western strategy. Most of the hard and quantitative questions that must be answered for the ultimate systems design and deployment decisions have to await future clarification in the light of the results of the SDI R&D strategic programme. However, we can begin the effort to understand how to assess strategic defences. This requires a clarification of their mission, an analysis of their qualitative aspects and how they might affect the competition between offence and defence, an understanding of Soviet policies on defences, their own as well as ours, and their probable reaction to the SDI. In particular will they refrain from BMD deployments if the US does?

How Effective Must Defences Be? How Should We Judge Them?

Must BMD protect people against Soviet forces and attack plans that have as their highest priority objective the massive destruction of innocent civilians? A positive answer implies that a less-than-leakproof defence is useless; it therefore poses formid-able and, according to many critics, insuper-able technological difficulties for BMD. The rush to judgment of the critics on this score flies in the face of abundant evidence that predicting technical impossibilities is a risky line of work. But even those who support defences would agree that the SDI would have to be viewed as a very high-risk venture if success in the R&D programme demanded nearly leak-proof effectiveness against a Soviet adversary determined to maintain at all costs the ability to destroy many of our largest cities and to use his forces in that way in the event of war.

The ability to provide a high level of protection against such an adversary was in fact the principal criterion for assessing the utility of BMD in the series of decisions beginning in 1967 and culminating in the ABM Treaty in 1972 – a criterion stemming from the MAD doctrine, that continues to prevail in much of the current discussion. This approach holds that to deter nuclear attack we must threaten deliberately to destroy innocent Soviet civilians; consequently deterrence depends only on the destructiveness of offensive nuclear forces used in retaliation for Soviet attack. A second and entirely distinct objective recognized but rejected in this conceptual framework is the ability to limit damage if the Soviet Union was actually to attack: namely to reduce the destruction of our own civilians by a combination of counterforce attacks, active defences and civil defence. Proponents of MAD viewed defences as irrelevant or unnecessary to deterrence except perhaps for their possible contribution to our ability to inflict 'unacceptable destruction' on Soviet Society by protecting our *Minuteman* missiles. (By and large, however, they opposed such a role for BMD as unnecessary during the debate preceding the signing of the ABM Treaty.) They also largely ignored the incredibility of relying on a suicidal response to deter Soviet attack and especially the incompatibility of such a strategy with Alliance guarantees.

Not least among the problems with accepting MAD as a strategic Commandment enshrined in the ABM Treaty, the Soviet leadership seems to have come from the mountain with a different set of tablets. They give no sign of recognizing MAD as holy writ. They merely note it, in an anthropological spirit, as a Western belief; and in a more manipulative way they exploit it as a doctrine that makes it easier for them to create political problems in the West.

What can replace MAD in Western strategic doctrine? To deter Soviet nuclear attack, we have to understand and work on the motives that might bring Soviet leaders to consider such an act. MAD appears to shortcut that necessity by relying on a response so terrible that it suffices to deter attack, whatever the motive and even if our response is avowedly suicidal and therefore inherently unlikely to be made. The rejection of MAD implies that we must make a closer examination of Soviet motivation for an attack and the contexts within which they might contemplate one.

Soviet leaders are most likely to consider the use of nuclear weapons if they are considering or are involved in serious non-nuclear military operations against the general purpose forces of one or more of the major Western Allies. Their incentives to initiate the use of nuclear weapons will depend on their assessment of their prospects in the conflict if they refrain and the likelihood and nature of Western response if they were to execute a nuclear attack.

Under such circumstances, Soviet doctrine and planning emphasize pre-emptive attacks to deny Western recourse to nuclear weapons. The survival of Western nuclear forces is therefore, as generally recognized, a primary factor in deterrence. But it is unlikely to be the only factor in the Soviet decision unless they confidently believe that they can virtually eliminate Western offensive forces or Western ability and will to use them. A 'bolt out of the blue' attack that leaves thousands of surviving SLBM warheads (not to mention bomber weapons and ICBM that survived an attack) is a very remote possibility.

Soviet doctrine emphasizes the goal of destroying opposing general purpose forces as quickly as possible to preclude the possibility of grave damage to the Soviet Union as a result of escalation. In regionally-confined conflicts, they might thus consider a limited nuclear strike to terminate a local military engagement that might otherwise spread or one that is going badly for them.

The targets of primary concern to the Soviet leaders would be military forces in the US or in theatres of operations – and most probably a combination of nuclear forces and those general purpose forces whose destruction promised to bring the conflict to a decisive and victorious conclusion. A set of particular significance, given the structure of NATO and its strategy, might be the facilities needed to support US reinforcement and resupply of Europe. The Soviet Union might reasonably expect that an early attack making timely reinforcement obviously infeasible would end concerted resistance in Europe.

With respect to damage to civilians, Soviet attitudes might range from indifference to a desire to avoid broadening the destruction while the West retained substantial retaliatory power to inflict widespread damage on the USSR. However, some of the targets that the Soviet leaders might endow with military significance are collocated with urban populations; as a result, an attack on their full target list could cause catastrophic civilian destruction. Widespread defences of the sort considered under SDI could substantially reduce such collateral damage.

If one holds such a view of Soviet motivation, denial of Soviet ability to achieve the specific military objectives of their attack would contribute powerfully to deterring attacks by them. The extent of such 'strategic denial' will depend on the effectiveness of defences.

How Effective Can Defences Be?
The Effects of New Technology
Technological advance since the 1960s offers the possibility of substantially different kinds of BMD systems from those we have considered in the past. While the 'Star Wars' image has focused attention on battle stations in space and directed-energy weapons, the relevant changes are a result of advances in a diverse set of technologies. Miniaturization of components permits mobility. Increasing precision in guidance through devices that home on the target allows us to consider non-nuclear warheads for defence interceptor missiles. Combination sensors and powerful information processing offers the possibility of distinguishing warheads from light-weight decoys outside the atmosphere. Air- or space-based defence platforms together with high performance and long-range surface-based interceptor missiles make it possible to intercept attacking missiles in all phases of their trajectory: boost phase – from launch to booster burn-out; early midcourse – from booster burn-out to completion of deployment of MIRV and exo-atmospheric decoys; late midcourse – from MIRV deployment to re-entry into the atmosphere; and terminal – from re-entry to detonation.

A multi-layer defence incorporating all of these elements would present very difficult problems for an attack planner, beginning in the boost phase when the missile is most vulnerable and a single intercept can destroy large numbers of MIRV. The most effective counter-measures against one layer will not, in general, be effective against others. The random attrition that attacking missiles would experience in early layers makes it much more difficult to concentrate forces on specific targets or to co-ordinate attacks designed to destroy or penetrate later layers.

From the defender's point of view, a multi-layer defence also allows several intercepts, providing the opportunity to compensate for single-shot probabilities (SSP) of successful intercept that are significantly less than unity. A defence that could destroy only half an attacking force in a single intercept, would, on the average, destroy almost 94% of the attack with four intercepts. Four intercepts each with an SSP of 0.7 would destroy more than 99% of the attack. If the later layers can determine which intercepts have been successful, and shoot only against the surviving attackers, the interceptor inventory required to obtain the benefits of multiple intercepts is greatly reduced. With an SSP of 0.5, the ability to 'shoot, look and shoot again' (S-L-S) reduces the inventory requirement, on the average, from four to less than 1.9 per attacker destroyed; with an SSP of 0.7 the requirement falls from four to less than 1.5.

These benefits might also be available to a degree in lesser combinations of layers or even within a single layer. A goal of SDI work on terminal defence is the ability to initiate intercept at high altitude. If such a defence had time to permit two shots at offensive warheads, it would raise the attrition rate to 91% for an SSP of 0.7.

The potential mobility of the terminal defences radically increases the difficulty of attacking the defence directly, a principal weakness of defences considered in the 1960s. Moreover, the radius of protection (the 'footprint') offered by the prospective terminal defence interceptors is far greater than in earlier terminal defence systems. Together, mobility and a large footprint may effectively prevent an attacker from concentrating his forces to exhaust the defence inventory by denying him the ability to assess the number of interceptors that might be assigned to protect any given target.

The ability of the defence to make the 'last move' permits it to allocate its forces to the protection of a specific (and, to the attacker, unknown) subset of a particular class of targets. For target sets where target redundancy forces the attacker to destroy a high proportion of the target set, this permits the defence to engage in a 'preferential' defence, greatly increasing the attacker's force requirements. While such a situation is inapplicable to the protection of civilians against the type of attack assumed in MAD, it is, or can be made relevant to several classes of military targets that would be an important element of a more realistic deterrent strategy. In planning our future forces, we can attempt to exploit the opportunities offered by a widespread territorial defence by 'designing' the military target system we present to a potential attacker.

Within the MAD context, defences must work almost perfectly to limit damage; the burden of uncertainty therefore falls on the defender. But in the context of a more realistic strategy for deterring attack, the burden of uncertainty falls instead on the attack planner. In assessing his ability to achieve the minimum level of attack effectiveness that might motivate a decision to attack, he will have to make assumptions about the effectiveness of defences and allocate his forces accordingly. If he underestimates, the outcome will be doubly disastrous because his attack plan will be poorly designed. He therefore has strong incentives to err on the side of conservatism, which will further increase the costs of overcoming the defences.

Efforts by the attacker to confuse or evade the defences have a long history, the upshot of which is that competition between offensive counter-measures such as decoys and jamming and defensive counter-counter-measures will not be decided early or once-and-for-all. The impact of new technology in this areas seems for the moment to be moving in favour of the defence against ballistic missiles (in contrast to the area of air defence), but the crystal ball is likely to remain changeable if not cloudy. Here again, conservatism is likely to limit the attack planner's confidence in the ability of clever and relatively cheap counter-measures, contributing to the deterrent value of defences.

The preceding discussion has focused on those aspects of technological change that improve the prospects for defences. Clearly, however, a number of problems remain.

The most serious of these is the vulnerability of defences to direct attack. This appears to be a problem particularly for space platforms in predictable and observable low earth orbits that regularly pass over Soviet territory. Though the terminal layer is not dependent on space-based assets, and though its vulnerability to direct attack appears to be much lower than earlier defence designs, it too cannot be assumed to be exempt from attacks on its air-based sensors, either single attacks or attacks spaced over time. The benefits of defences that were discussed above would not accrue to a defence that could be destroyed easily and reliably by the Soviet Union before or during an attack. The vulnerability of defences must therefore remain a major concern during the R&D conducted under the SDI.

In the debate over BMD before the ABM Treaty, opponents listed among the problems for such defences the requirement to release authority to fire defensive weapons within the short warning time available in a ballistic missile attack. Since the defences then under consideration depended on nuclear warheads, such criticisms carried substantial weight in the debate. If the SDI eliminates the need for nuclear weapons, this issue will be far less acute.

Supporters of MAD have also argued that defences are destabilizing in crises for two reasons: first, they assert that protection of people reduces deterrence of nuclear war by reducing its horror; second, the greater effectiveness of defences against an offensive force disrupted by pre-launch attrition allegedly increases the difference in the damage incurred in striking first rather than being struck.

Such arguments ignore the stabilizing effect of defences in reducing the ability of Soviet

missiles. Extreme precision also makes it possible to consider conventional warheads for specialized long-range attack tasks, enhancing deterrence by providing effective, discriminate and credible responses to attacks against which a full nuclear response would be suicidal and hence incredible. From the point of view of verification of arms agreements, however, such systems must be considered as dual-capable. Missiles with the range, payload and accuracy to perform a useful task with a non-nuclear warhead would clearly be effective with a lighter and much more lethal nuclear warhead. These developments will pose insuperable problems for arms agreements unless the parties can tolerate a growing degree of imprecision in their ability to verify the size of the opposing missile force. Ballistic missile defences can help in this respect by reducing the sensitivity of the balance to illegal nuclear missiles.

It is too early to reach definitive conclusions about the effects of ballistic missile defence deployments on the prospects for useful arms agreements. On the whole, however, such deployments appear more likely than not to improve those prospects by comparison with the dismal record to date and the equally dismal current outlook.

NOTES

[1] *Aviation Week*, 16 January 1984, pp. 14–16.
[2] *Ibid.*

The 'Star Wars' Debate: The Western Alliance and Strategic Defence: Part II

PROF. LAWRENCE FREEDMAN

I call upon the scientific community in our country, those who gave us nuclear weapons, to turn their talents now to the cause of mankind and world peace, to give us the means of rendering these nuclear weapons impotent and obsolete.[1]

If these words are to be taken seriously, then 23 March 1983 will be taken as the date when a revolution in contemporary strategic affairs was set in motion. President Reagan committed his government to the overthrow of the entrenched and domineering offence that has reigned supreme in nuclear matters since 1945 and has exercised an overbearing influence on international affairs. The age of the defence is dawning. Mutual Assured Destruction (MAD) must prepare to give way to Assured Survival.

For such a revolutionary declaration, the President's speech was something of a curiosity. It was not the result of any major analytical effort within government nor the subject of consultations with allies. The origins appear to lie with lobbies as exotic as the technologies they promote. When the bureaucracy was tasked to get to work to bring about the new strategic order, they did so in such a slow and confused manner that it was soon robbed of many of its revolutionary credentials.

There was certainly a revolution in method. We have become used to the idea that in the modern world technology leads doctrine. Here strategic requirements were put to the fore which the scientists and engineers were then charged to meet. This was despite the fact that the necessary technology was well beyond the current state of the art and the weight of scientific opinion appeared to be that the President's utopian goal would remain far out of reach. Even if all went

according to plan, the new strategic order was unlikely to arrive until well into the next century.

Most successful revolutions are better prepared than this and run more clearly with the tide of history. The full implications of what is now known as the Strategic Defense Initiative (SDI) do not appear to have been particularly well thought out prior to its launch. Given the lack of enthusiasm in Congress and in the bureaucracy, it may well now peter out of its own accord. However, it also has a substantial measure of popular support, a large number of research contracts have been awarded and the effort has now got some central direction from within the Pentagon.

The notion that it would be both more moral and prudent to concentrate on defence rather than on a destructive offence has been around from the earliest days of the nuclear age and can be expected to retain some popularity and influence even if the current initiative lapses. The fact that the concept of strategic defence has managed to reach centre stage – if only for a short time – provides us at the least with an opportunity to discuss its merits and failings.

In what follows I will talk about the SDI rather than 'Star Wars'. SDI is not only the official term but is also more descriptive. The President did not actually mention space-based systems in his speech – they were mentioned in the associated White House briefing. It was inevitable that anything in this area would attract this sort of label – indeed it had already been applied to discussions of anti-satellite (ASAT) weapons and the two are still confused together. In the same way similar projects two decades ago attracted the 'Buck Rogers' label.

It is impossible to discuss this subject without being drawn into a number of technical debates. I will touch on these debates without exploring the various systems being proposed. As I will argue later, the basic question is whether or not there is a shift under way in favour of the defence at the expense of the offence and there seems to be less dispute than one might imagine that there is not. Furthermore, the preoccupation with the efficacy or otherwise of high-technology systems distracts attention from the more basic questions concerning the objectives of strategic defence and their desirability should they prove to be feasible.[2]

Background

In the past the idea that a nation should do its best to protect itself against all forms of attack would not have been considered revolutionary; indeed, to suggest anything to the contrary would have seemed somewhat bizarre, even treacherous.

What has persuaded policy-makers of the limited value of defences against nuclear attack is the high cost of even the smallest failure, and the continuing success of the offence in coming up with new measures to trump any attempts to establish an effective defence.

As the United States began to consider her vulnerability to attack from the Soviet Union, there was a natural inclination to explore the possibilities for defence. In 1952 President Truman created a special subcommittee of the National Security Council (NSC) to consider the Soviet ability to injure the United States. This subcommittee reported in May 1953 to the new Eisenhower Administration with rather gloomy conclusions. The lack of an ability to protect the United States from a nuclear attack was deemed by the NSC to constitute an 'unacceptable risk to our nation's survival'. Complete invulnerability was recognised to be impossible but 'a reasonably effective defense system can and must be obtained'.[3] By 1960 some $20 billion had been spent on the development of an air defence system that was about to be rendered virtually obsolete by ICBM.

This experience did not deter advocates of an anti-ballistic missile defence but it made the US government more wary of committing large sums of money to measures to defend cities from an all-out Soviet attack. At best ABM were seen to be useful in protecting high-value military targets or in acting against small-scale attacks such as might be posed from China. During the 1960s the United States came to the conclusion that the best method of deterring a nuclear attack on the United States was the threat of retaliation in kind. This view appeared to have been accepted by the Soviet Union when she joined the United States in signing the 1972 ABM Treaty. The prevailing view was summed up by Secretary of Defense James Schlesinger in 1974 when arguing in favour of cutting air defences:

> Since we cannot defend our cities against strategic missiles, there is nothing to be gained by trying to defend them against a relatively small force of strategic bombers. I am sure the Soviet leaders understand that an attack on our cities, whether by bombers or missiles, would inevitably result in the destruction of their cities.[4]

There were always objectors in the strategic studies community to this view.[5] During the 1970s the critics grew in strength. Their main target, however, was not the view that nothing could be done to protect populations from nuclear attack but that the only option available to the West in initiating nuclear exchanges would be all-out attacks on cities. If there was criticism of the restrictions on ABM, it was that this denied one option for protecting land-based missiles.[6]

The Reagan Administration came to power less than well disposed towards the 1972 ABM Treaty. There were dark hints that abrogation might be necessary at the time of the 1982 review of the Treaty. In the debate over the basing of the MX (*Peacekeeper*) ICBM, ABM were canvassed as potentially valuable complements to some of the proposed schemes. However, the Administration could not bring itself to threaten to abrogate the Treaty in order to save MX. It is worth noting that, even when announcing the *Densepack* basing mode for MX in November 1982 (which was also the time of the US–Soviet review of the ABM Treaty), the

President clearly disassociated this system from a ballistic missile defence despite the widespread view that such a defence was needed to make it work.

Because ABM technology was discussed largely in the context of the survival of US land-based ICBM, it did not appear central to the Administration's attempts to wrest US strategy away from the grip of assured destruction. This attempt was largely based on changes to targeting plans and developments of more sophisticated offensive systems. This is not the place to review the Administration's efforts in the area of strategic doctrine. Suffice it to say that the efforts to build on the Carter Administration's countervailing strategy and plan for 'prolonged' nuclear wars have failed to convince. The main result was to stimulate adverse reaction at home and abroad, and some substantial critiques by analysts concerned with both the inner logic of the doctrine and the practicality of conducting a nuclear war along the lines envisaged.

Assured destruction was criticized as a strategic doctrine for failing to provide the United States with options other than the mass destruction of civilians in the event of nuclear hostilities (a crime of which it was not actually guilty). To the critics, the failure was compounded by the unwillingness of the Soviet Union to limit its plans in this manner. The resultant debate revolved around what damage the US might need in order to inflict upon the Soviet Union rather than what the Soviet Union might do to the US and the West in general. This was quite reasonable, given that it is the West that is presumed to be the most dependent on a credible nuclear strategy. The difficulty was that, whatever the offensive tactics that might be developed for the West, the problem of the character of any Soviet retaliation and the form taken by later nuclear exchanges – leading to mutual assured destruction – remained.

In the end, if the Administration was serious about its commitment to escape from the grim logic of MAD, then it had to get round its critics' fundamental argument – that MAD was not just a policy choice but was a fact of life in the modern world. If only the Soviet second-strike capability could be undermined, then US strategy would gain a formidable credibility. In this sense the President's speech represented the logical conclusion of the search for a credible nuclear strategy that has occupied US policy-makers since Robert McNamara's days as Secretary of Defense.[7]

Two Steps Forward

There were no hints that a revolution was being prepared in the White House in the first months of 1983. In the discussions within the Scowcroft Commission attempting to forge a bipartisan policy on strategic forces, the potential benefits of BMD were not seen to extend much beyond the protection of land-based missiles. The Commission's Report (released *after* the President's 23 March speech) concluded:

> Applications of current technology offer no real promise of being able to defend the United States against massive nuclear attack in this century . . . At this time . . . the Commission believes that no ABM technologies appear to combine practicality, survivability, low cost, and technical effectiveness sufficiently to justify proceeding beyond the stage of technology development.[8]

A continued research programme was deemed necessary just in case there was a need to respond to a Soviet 'breakout' from the constraints of the ABM Treaty.

This sense that any collapse of the ABM Treaty would be at the instigation of the Soviet Union and not the United States seemed to be in line with Administration thinking. Less and less was heard about the review of the ABM Treaty as it grew closer. Official policy, as outlined in a Presidential Statement of November 1982, stated that the United States did

> not wish to embark on any course of action that could endanger the current ABM Treaty so long as it is observed by the Soviet Union.

There were no plans to deploy any BMD system, even that permitted under the 1972

Treaty, but research would continue on the relevant technology. The objectives of this research effort were:

stability for our ICBM in the nineties, a hedge against Soviet breakout of the ABM Treaty, and the technical competence to evaluate Soviet ABM developments.[9]

These objectives were broadly similar to those of the Carter Administration.[10] The positive interest was confined to protection of ICBM silos; otherwise the only requirement was to be ready to respond to any initiative taken by the Soviet Union.

The new policy was announced by the President in his speech of 23 March[11] and elaborated further in background briefings and in supporting statements, speeches and interviews by the President and his senior officials, particularly Secretary of Defense Caspar Weinberger and Science Adviser Dr George Keyworth.

The key features of the new policy were as follows:

- It was self-consciously revolutionary and visionary. In his speech the President described an 'ultimate goal' of eliminating the threat posed by nuclear weapons. A few days later he spoke of his initiative as offering an alternative to one in which 'the great nations of the world will sit here like people facing themselves across a table each with a cocked gun, and no one knowing whether someone might tighten the finger on the trigger'.[12]
- Assured destruction would be turned on its head: people and not weapons were to be protected; weapons and not people were to be threatened. The objectives went well beyond guarding against Soviet first strikes or protecting offensive missiles.
- The system would provide total and not just partial protection. As Caspar Weinberger put it: 'The defensive systems the President is talking about are not designed to be partial. What we want to try to get is a system which will develop a defense that is thoroughly reliable and total ... I don't see any reason why that can't be done'.[13]

- It was specifically concerned with 'strategic ballistic missiles' (the only weapons mentioned in the original speech). This aspect appears to rest uneasily with the need for total protection. However the argument was that ballistic missiles posed the most critical test to any defence and, if they could be stopped, then slower-moving forces would pose far less of a challenge.[14]
- The protection would be extended to allies. The President's 'vision' was to 'intercept and destroy strategic ballistic missiles before they reached our own soil or that of our allies'. This statement implies a wider (if not wholly inappropriate) definition of a strategic missile than is normally adopted by the United States. Unfortunately elsewhere in the same speech the President referred to intermediate nuclear force, confirming the impression that the inclusion of allies was something of an after thought.
- At least for the time being, the 1972 ABM Treaty would be respected. The Treaty permitted research, and deployment decisions were years away.
- The objective was 'neither military superiority nor political advantage'. Indeed, in a later press conference, the President suggested that, when the defensive system was developed, one option would be to pass the technology on to the Soviet Union. Secretary Weinberger stated that: 'I would hope and assume that the Soviets with all the work they have done and are doing in this field, would develop a similar defense, which would have the effect of totally and completely removing these missiles from the face of the earth'.[15]

One Step Back

Since the spring of 1983 the policy has been revised substantially and is in a number of respects now reverting back to the sort of rationales adopted prior to March 1983. Instead of the SDI being presented as a self-conscious piece of doctrinal revisionism, it is increasingly being described as a prudent response to an initiative already undertaken by the Soviet Union. Even more significantly, although the objective of a population defence has not been disavowed, the basic objective has now reverted back to the protection of US military capabilities against a Soviet first strike. In May 1984 Secretary Weinberger observed that:

SDI does not preclude any intermediate deployment that could provide, among other things, defense of the offensive deterrent forces which, of course, we still have to maintain.[16]

As this quotation also illustrates, there is now no pretence that it will prove possible to eliminate offensive weapons as a result of this initiative – at least until the ultimate goal is within reach.

The revisionism may even have moved a stage further. Lt-General James Abrahamson, directing the SDI, told reporters in May 1984 that:

My specific charge is to ensure that possibility of early deployments in case there is a breakout of the Anti-Ballistic Missile Treaty on the part of the Russians.[17]

Some proponents of strategic defence now find it very hard to imagine that the President ever even considered the idea of defending civilians, although he clearly did.[18]

This more modest tendency has been reflected in the actual development of the SDI. National Security Study Directive (NSSD) 6-83 required an examination of the technology that could eliminate the threat posed by nuclear ballistic missiles to the security of the United States and her allies. A Defensive Technologies Study, headed by Dr James C. Fletcher, and a Future Security Strategy Study, headed by Fred Hoffman, reported in October 1983. These studies were integrated in an interagency group report. The essential conclusion of the Fletcher Panel was that 'a robust, multitiered ballistic missile defense system can eventually be made to work'. The stress, however, was on the 'eventually'. This was a matter for long-term research.[19] This approach angered a number of the more enthusiastic advocates of strategic defence.[20] In his National Security Decision Directive

(NSDD) of 6 January 1984 the President sided with the more cautious approach and called for 'initiation of a focused program to demonstrate the technical feasibility of enhancing deterrence and thereby reducing the risk of nuclear war through greater reliance on defensive technology'.[21] To the press, key officials stressed the long-term and speculative nature of the programme.[22] In late March, Lt-General Abrahamson was appointed to direct the SDI. With a certain amount of bureaucratic friction, Abrahamson's office began to pull together a number of disparate BMD-related programmes from around the Department of Defense.

As things stand, the SDI is concerned with long-term research rather than medium-term deployment. The proposals of those in lobbies such as 'High Frontier' for a move to early deployment based on available technology have been rejected on the familiar grounds of overestimated performance and underestimated cost. Known but unfashionable technologies such as nuclear ABM are being discarded and, while a short-term capacity to respond to a Soviet breakout from the ABM Treaty is being maintained, it is not being taken much further. In long-term research the easier technologies are being kept for later while priority is given to the most challenging problems, especially laser technology and the computational capabilities necessary to manage large-scale defences. The assumption is that a layered defence, threatening the offence at the boost, post-boost, midcourse and terminal phases will be necessary to ensure against excessive leakage at any one layer. The effort remains directed at ballistic missiles. While a system capable of dealing with ICBM can also deal with intermediate-range systems (although not necessarily using multiple layers), the problems of dealing with bombers and cruise missiles are quite different.

There appears to be some debate within the Administration as to the need or the desirability of combining an effort to deal with the 'air-breathing threat' with that to deal with strategic ballistic missiles. According to one school of thought, it is by no means clear that in the future (as in the past) bombers and cruise missiles will pose far simpler defensive problems. They do not leave rocket flares at boost stage to allow them to be detected at launch nor do they re-enter the atmosphere. Although their speed is slower than missiles, they are even now difficult to detect by radar and with 'stealth' technology this will be still more difficult in the future. Some proponents of SDI have argued that 'air-breathers' are more stable than missiles because of their slower speed. A Mr William Furniss of the Pentagon has been quoted as suggesting, rather curiously, that if the strategic competition were pushed back towards bombers it 'would get us back to the relatively stable period of the 1950s'. However, it is hard to see how ballistic missile defences could remain credible with an unrestricted bomber and cruise missile threat. To state one obvious problem, ground-based components of the defence would be vulnerable to a pre-emptive cruise missile attack. As Major-General John A. Shard of the USAF put it: 'If you're going to fix the roof, you don't want to leave the doors and windows open'.[23] Current funding for both development and procurement of air defence systems is only a fraction of that on the SDI.

The current plan is for the research phase to be completed early in the 1990s when decisions will have to be taken on whether or not to enter systems development, when prototypes of actual systems are to be designed, built and tested. This will be followed by a transition stage during which there will be 'incremental, sequential deployment of defensive systems' to be followed by a final phase of deployments of high-effective, multiphased defensive systems. It may be another thirty years before this final phase is completed.[24]

The eventual cost remains a matter of conjecture. Current spending is quite modest although it is projected to rise significantly over the coming four years.[25] Richard De Lauer, Under Secretary of Defense for Research and Engineering, has warned that deployment costs will be 'staggering', and suggested that the cost over ten years of deployment would be equivalent to that currently being spent on offensive arms – some 14% of the total budget each year. In current dollars this would amount to a total of some \$400–450 bn.[26] This would be after substantial development costs.

More seriously it does not include the costs of introducing parallel defences against bombers and cruise missiles.[27] Furthermore, there can be no expectation of compensating savings in offensive arms. Indeed, it is not inconceivable that there will be increased expenditures on offensive arms to meet the challenges posed by the introduction of Soviet defences. Clearly therefore a substantial amount of new money is going to have to be found if these schemes are to come to fruition. Already there are signs that those responsible for other aspects of US defences are worried that their programmes will be crowded out by SDI.[28]

Ends

The most important development has been the shift away from the protection of civilians as the prime objective of the programme. After the President's speech, Congressional supporters tabled a People Protection Act to:

> implement the call of the President for a national strategy seeking to protect people from nuclear war and to render nuclear weapons obsolete.

They must now feel as if they had succumbed to a life insurance salesman only to discover that the policy only covered the car. We have already noted the move to 'intermediate' objectives involving the defence of high-value military targets. As Lt-General Abrahamson has now explained: 'A perfect astrodome defense is not a realistic thing'.[29] Supporters of this move argue that it is genuinely intermediate in that it will provide opportunities to prove technologies essential to the more ambitious schemes and that it will be possible to move to a complete defence through the addition of extra layers. However, this pushes the President's objective even further into the background.[30] It also means that some of the more difficult policy issues may have to be faced earlier than would have been the case had the SDI concentrated on research in areas critical to population defence.

The intermediate objectives have long been associated with ballistic missile defence:

- *Hard-point defence.* Protection of land-based missiles and command-and-control centres against a Soviet first strike has always been a favoured rationale for ABM.
- *Strategy-denial.* A more sophisticated variant of hard-point defence points to the concentration in Soviet strategy on a variety of forms of counterforce targeting in the conduct of campaigns against Western Europe as well as the United States. By denying the Soviet Union preferred strategic options, it will be deterred from engaging in any nuclear operations.
- *Protection against small attacks.* Even if the system cannot deal with a massive assault it should be able to deal with accidental launches of missiles or smaller nuclear forces.
- *Damage limitation.* By reducing the total number of warheads detonated, the damage to civilian life and property can be reduced though it would still be very high. It has even been suggested that strategic defences offer one way of staving off the 'nuclear winter' by keeping the number of warheads detonated beneath the threshold that might trigger a climatic catastrophe.[31]

The Administration has insisted that the fundamental purpose is to enhance deterrence, and this is particularly clear with regard to the first two objectives listed above. With regard to protection against small attacks, it is only China that could conceivably pose a ballistic missile threat to the United States. It would be somewhat ironic if the anti-China rationale which was deemed to be rather feeble when adopted by Secretary of Defense McNamara in 1967 was resurrected now. For the moment, it is the Soviet Union which will find this rationale most appealing. As for damage limitation, the Administration is sensitive to the suggestion that it is preparing for war and has tended to play this down.[32]

There are, in addition, three subsidiary benefits that might result from continuing with a substantial research effort which did not reach any definite conclusion:

- *Response to breakout.* Maintaining the capability to respond to a Soviet breakout from the constraints imposed by the ABM Treaty tends to be supported even by those who object to the SDI.[33]
- *Bargaining chip.* The prospect of a successful US deployment of an effective defence will encourage the Soviet Union to take arms control more seriously.[34]
- *Diversion of resources.* In order to deal with developing US defensive capabilities, the Soviet Union will be forced to direct resources into improving her offensive counter-measures.

It should be noted with regard to these subsidiary benefits that they still depend on there being a reasonable possibility that the primary objectives can be obtained. For example, the bargaining chip argument is normally taken to suggest that reductions on offensive arms will be easier to obtain as the Soviet Union recognizes the futility of persevering with offensive arms in the face of ever-more-impressive US defences. However, if US defences fail to impress then no negotiating leverage is provided at all, except possibly in encouraging further restrictions on the defence.

Nor would there be much point in responding to a breakout from Treaty constraints with a comparable defensive build-up if the resultant defences were likely to be ineffective. The Soviet Union has been more energetic in the past with both air defences and ABM: the US response has been to strengthen the offence.

In its original form the President's initiative was vulnerable to the standard criticisms made against similar proposals in the past. The first side to achieve an effective defence would put the other at a considerable disadvantage. The other would have advance notice of this shift in the strategic balance and might be tempted to pre-empt before the shift had become absolute. So the transition period would be one of immense strain, and indeed the problem of transition will be stressful if any serious change in the existing strategic order is contemplated. Once the new defences were in place then the favoured side might be tempted to exploit its advantage during a crisis by launching a nuclear strike in the expectation (which might turn out to have been disastrously misguided) that it would receive nothing in return.

These rather grand strategic problems are now somewhat pushed into the background, along with the objective of 'people protection'. The SDI will achieve less than originally envisaged and so, by the same token, is less potentially destabilizing than its detractors have suggested. Most important of all, the 'intermediate' objectives do not take us out of the condition of mutually assured destruction. An opponent determined to inflict unacceptable damage could still do so. In principle these objectives are perfectly consistent with 1960s-vintage strategic doctrine.

Indeed their most likely effect is to reinforce a concentration on city-targeting. As any defence would have some damage-limiting capacity, the Soviet Union might feel obliged to compensate by improving her area-attack capabilities to guard against any diminuition in the 'ultimate' threat. Furthermore, to the extent that the United States succeeded in denying to Soviet planners lucrative military targets, the planners would have little choice but to stress 'soft' targets such as cities. There seems to be some attempt by supporters of SDI to suggest that this does not matter because of a lack of Soviet interest in counter-city targeting. This argument is hard to take seriously. It is particularly difficult to imagine any President taking it seriously during a crisis or in the early stages of war.[35]

It is certainly the case that Soviet doctrine puts a lot of stress on counterforce targeting, but the conviction with which this is done can easily be exaggerated. Furthermore, this approach is most relevant to the European theatre where the problems of protecting military assets are much more severe. It is important to deny the Soviet Union a first-strike capability, but they are nowhere near achieving such a capability at the moment. The problems of land-based missile survivability are acute but that is not the case with sea-based systems and strategic defence is irrelevant to the problems of anti-submarine warfare. It has to be asked how much expense

and bother the 'intermediate' objectives are worth. As strategic problems they may not be as urgent as suggested by those proposing the SDI as a solution. Any major deployment of strategic defences will add to Soviet uncertainties about what she can get away with and so to some extent reinforce deterrence. However, it is doubtful that the increment of deterrence will have been worth the price, especially if other elements of the force structure have declined as a result of the diversion of resources to SDI.

A definition of the objectives of SDI which might be considered neutral might be: 'the progressive elimination of offensive nuclear options through the application of defensive technologies'. This definition raises the question of which side is likely to benefit most from the denial of targeting options. In the past it has been the West rather than the East that is believed to have been most in need of a credible nuclear strategy. Unless the advocates presume that the Soviet Union will not be able to follow a US breakout, which would require a considerable act of faith and contradict their own statements on the advanced stage of Soviet research and development, then it must be expected that Western options will also be reduced. Contrary to the received wisdom, the presumption behind much of the advocacy of the SDI appears to be that the Soviet Union is in the greatest need of nuclear options. We find George Keyworth suggesting that the great advantage of SDI in the long-term will be 'to enforce retaliation as the sole rationale for nuclear delivery systems.'[36]

This is by no means an unreasonable objective, but it contradicts NATO's current position that it is most in need of a threat of nuclear escalation to deter aggression. The response by the US Administration, and other Western governments, to proposals to remove nuclear weapons from strategic calculations in Europe through 'no-first-use' declarations has been that this would make Europe 'safe for conventional warfare'. Presumably this objection applies to the same effect being achieved through the neutralization of both sides' offensive nuclear weapons. The introduction of effective defences therefore could reduce the risks surrounding conventional operations – the very area where the Warsaw Pact is believed to enjoy its most significant advantages. Even if the result of both sides protecting vital military assets was to reduce the opportunities for sophisticated nuclear operations, according to the conventional wisdom in NATO the Alliance has most to lose from such a development. It may well be that we would be better off if neither side had the ability to mount such operations at any nuclear level. The point is that the SDI only appears to be improving the position if it presumes that NATO's fundamental problem – the incredibility of the threat to use nuclear weapons first – has already been dealt with by other measures. To stabilize strategic relations on this new basis, the SDI would have to be accompanied by a major improvement in conventional defences.

Allies
This brings us to the whole question of the impact of all of this on the Alliance. The Allies were not consulted about the 23 March speech and their response has been muted to say the least. The initial reaction was simply to hope that the speech was an aberration and that there would be no significant follow-through. This is still the hope but no longer the expectation. In addition to briefing teams sent round to NATO capitals, Defense Secretary Caspar Weinberger gave a briefing to Ministers at the Nuclear Planning Group meeting in Turkey in early April. This seems to have had a negative reception and was followed by the West Germans expressing their doubts publicly. The French, after initially toying with the idea of developing their own defensive systems (in line with the established practice of asserting that France can follow any new technological line should she so desire), have now become quite hostile and have even tabled a proposal at the Geneva Committee on Disarmament that would prohibit space-based defences. With the British they are particularly concerned about the impact on their national nuclear deterrent. Alliance concern reportedly led to consultations in Washington in July 1984.[37]

In addition to the special concerns of the British and French, there have been more general concerns expressed about the effect of the SDI on arms control and strategic stability. While supporters of the Initiative argue that an effective defence would render the US nuclear guarantee to Europe much more credible, the European concern has been that the overall effect would be 'de-coupling'. Either Europe would remain extremely vulnerable and so be kept hostage by the Soviet Union, or else the United States, now safe and sound behind her protective shield, would withdraw from her international commitments.

The Administration has sought to ease these concerns largely by insisting that the protective shield would indeed extend to Western Europe. Having already promised to do one impossible thing why not promise another? There is every indication that the promise was made lightly. There has been no discussion of how, if at all, the Allies would contribute to either the construction or the costs of such a system. While it is the case that the ability to intercept during the boost phase would provide some defence against medium- and intermediate-range missiles, the shorter flight time is certain to limit what might be achieved by multiple layers and the sheer diversity of threats faced by Western Europe (especially those Allies bordering the Warsaw Pact) would threaten to overwhelm all defences.

Again, of course, more modest objectives for the SDI change the debate. The problems faced by the British and French remain and one can expect their anxiety levels to grow the more it looks like the ABM Treaty is close to collapse. But otherwise, the fact that there is unlikely to be real invulnerability for the United States means that there is less need to worry about 'Fortress America'. This does not of course mean that that the Europeans will stop worrying along these lines.[38] The most significant result of the shift to the more limited objectives (and one that does not seem to be fully appreciated in Europe) is that it puts the promise of extending strategic defence to Europe in a completely different light.

There are a large number of military targets of interest to the Soviet Union in Europe. Protection against air attack is already considered necessary for many, so protection against missile attack could be seen as a natural complement. Furthermore, tactical anti-ballistic missiles (TABM) are not directly prohibited by the ABM Treaty, and their deployment would therefore have fewer international repercussions than strategic defences. Furthermore, there is already a candidate for a TABM in the *Patriot* missile which is near deployment in an air defence role.[39] It would be ironic if an initiative that began stressing the defence of the American people against strategic ballistic missiles ended up proving extra protection for military installations in Europe!

Patriot reveals more about the problems than the possibilities of strategic defence. The current bill to introduce it to perform its primary air defence role is $11 bn. Testing has been disappointing and the current expectation is that deployment may not be complete until the 1990s.[40] Furthermore, as one proponent of TABM has warned:

I don't think we can afford the numbers required. . . . One response by the Soviet Union would be to MIRV the front-end of their heavy tactical missile systems, which would stress any TABM system.[41]

Means
We come next to the whole question of the feasibility of the attempt to introduce effective defences. The SDI controversy has been a gift to disputatious scientists and therefore rather forbidding to the non-scientist. But it is also the case that the scientific debate is highly speculative since no specific systems have as yet been adopted. Lt-General Abrahamson has complained that many of the critics of SDI are 'creating an Edsel and then going back and shooting it down'.[42] They have, of course, nothing else to aim at for the moment. It may also be the case that the critics are still attacking the President's original concept rather than the one that is now guiding the bureaucracy.

The President's original speech was not made on the basis of any new technological assessments,[43] and we have noted the lack of enthusiasm in the initial reactions of the responsible figures in the Pentagon. The Fletcher Report's endorsement of the Initiative was cautious, certainly too cautious for many of the SDI's more enthusiastic proponents.[44]

It is generally agreed that the fundamental question behind the technical arguments is whether or not a trend is under way to shift the advantage from the offence to the defence in the long-standing duel between the two. It is also generally agreed that there is no firm evidence as yet that such a shift is under way. However, one proponent of the SDI, Robert Jastrow, has argued that the shift has already been developed as far as point defence goes. It will, he argues, cost twice as much to counter the defence as to build it.[45]

It is necessary to examine this argument very carefully. The equation for the offence–defence duel does not just involve weighing the cost of protecting an individual target against the cost of penetrating that defence. It is also necessary to put into the equation the value of the target being protected. As point defence is designed to protect high-value military assets, then its failure might be decisive – in which case this is what is going to matter much more to the enemy than the cost of the offence or the defence.

Second, the defence costs include protecting assets that may be important but which the enemy has no intention of attacking. The more complete the defence the more there is going to be wasted effort. If it is desired, on the other hand, to protect only a few critical installations then the offence–defence duel may only be a small part of the total battle and so the relative costs will be relatively unimportant and outweighed by the value of the installations themselves.

Third, because of the problems of lead times, the defence has to anticipate possible changes in the offence which might be different from those that the offence chooses to make. It is being suggested that this time the penalty may be the other way round in that the offence will need to prepare countermeasures before it can be sure that any particular defensive problem will actually materialize. By following a number of defensive possibilities in research, the USSR will be forced to hedge against a wide range of possible developments. The Pentagon has argued:

If, for example, the Soviets persisted in attempts to expand their massive offensive forces, a flexible research and development program would force Soviet planners to adopt counter-measures, increasing the costs of their offensive buildup and reducing their flexibility in designing new forces in a manner that they would prefer.[46]

So, in addition to arguing that the past cost advantage favouring the defence is to be relinquished, it is also argued that the lead-time advantage is also to pass to the defence. It does not as yet seem evident why this should be so. It would be surprising if the Soviet Union was already doing much more than tentative research herself in response to the SDI and, given the enormous amount of time needed to even deploy the sort of systems envisaged, there seems no reason for the Russians not to bide their time until American plans become clear.

This relates to a more general proposition that only holds if things can be truly shown to be moving the way of the defence. It has been asserted that the development of an impressive defence will force the Soviet Union to stop investing in offensive missiles and thus serve the cause of stability. In the 'transition phase', as outlined by Lt-General Abrahamson in May 1984, it is envisaged that:

> as the US and Soviet Union deploy defenses against ballistic missiles that progressively reduce the value of such missiles, significant reductions in nuclear ballistic missiles would be negotiated and implemented.[47]

Elsewhere, he has made it clear that he envisages a downgrading of Soviet offences as a natural response to the progress of the SDI.[48] But if in practice it is nuclear ballistic missiles that are still reducing the value of strategic defences, and there has yet to be anything other than an assertion that the reverse is likely to be true, what does that mean for the new initiative?

There seems no reason to believe that the Soviet Union will not continue to invest in offensive arms. She has shown herself in the past, perhaps foolishly, willing to resist technological trends. When the offence was clearly in the ascendant, she still invested heavily in defences. It would be surprising if in the face of the SDI she meekly bowed to US technological supremacy and provided the US with a strategic walkover.[49]

The SDI only looks promising so long as the offensive problem is not allowed to get out of hand.[50] Two judgments are worth quoting on this issue. The first is that of James Thomson of the Rand Corporation on the basis of an extensive project conducted on strategic defences with full access to classified information. In testimony to Congress he considered whether the offence or the defence would have the economic advantage in an arms race:

> We concluded that the offense would have the advantage. This advantage became overwhelming if we were attempting to protect populations to a very high level of effectiveness, or what might be called near leak-proof defenses. At lower levels of protection, the offense still had an advantage, but not so pronounced.[51]

The second is that of James Fletcher himself:

> The ultimate utility, effectiveness, cost, complexity and degree of technical risk in this system will depend not only on the technology itself, but also on the extent to which the Soviet Union either agrees to mutual defense arrangements or offensive limitations.[52]

Arms Control

The SDI may well be dependent on a prior agreement limiting offensive arms. The continued lack of progress in START poses the problem of an unconstrained offence. But if the SDI succeed without the sort of arms control that we currently lack, it cannot prosper with the sort of arms control that we currently have.

It cannot move beyond the research stage without abrogation of the 1972 Treaty. Those wishing to stop the SDI need take no exceptional arms-control measures. Their task is only to ensure compliance with the current provisions. This, of course, is easier said than done, given that it is difficult to draw the line between research and development and between ABM and the related anti-aircraft and anti-satellite technologies.[53] If both sides step up their strategic defence activities then the Treaty is going to be put under severe strain, even if there is no formal abrogation. Furthermore, the question of unambiguous violation may arise sooner rather than later as a result of the need to test critical components. A 'demonstration test' would be a highly risky venture if it could only be undertaken after rejection of the Treaty but without any confidence that it would lead to a successful system. The only possible area where deployment might be permitted would be with TABM and here there would be problems if it were designed to deal with systems of any significant range, because it would also be able to deal with SLBM. It may also be the case that the development of anti-satellite technology (ASAT) provides opportunities to develop components of ABM without doing so directly, although these tests may be sufficiently direct to lead to charges that the ABM Treaty is being violated.[54] Equally, recent developments in mid-course interception systems are of value in the development of ASAT. It is therefore likely that an ASAT treaty would impede the SDI.

This to some extent would depend on the nature of the systems banned under an ASAT treaty. Current thinking in the Administration appears to be that low altitude systems cannot be verified and therefore should be excluded. If only high-altitude systems were banned, while this might interfere with development in the short- and medium-term, in the long-term it might help the SDI because it would alleviate a critical vulnerability of any system dependent on space-based components.

For the same reasons that the Administration might prefer an arms-control regime that allowed unconstrained defensive deployments and a highly restricted offence, the Soviet Union is unlikely to provide them with such a regime. The linkage between offensive and defensive arms control is well established, and has always been stressed by the United States. At the time of the 1972 Treaty, the US issued a unilateral statement to the effect that she would reconsider her support for the Treaty without a later Treaty on offensive arms, and this position was apparently reiterated in the run-up to the 1982 Review Conference (although it was hardly the Soviet Union that was responsible then for the lack of a Treaty on Offensive Arms).[55] The linkage is now likely to be played back at the United States. Any treaty on offensive arms will depend on continued adherence to the ABM Treaty. The same is likely with an ASAT treaty. Soviet, and for that matter French, proposals against the 'militarization' of space are clearly designed to get at both the SDI and ASAT. While it has been the American attempt to link discussion of ASAT with offensive weapons that has gained most of the publicity in the squabbling over the agenda for the proposed September 1984 Vienna talks, there was also an American desire to separate ASAT from SDI. Those promoting SDI are clearly anxious that any early agreement in this area could abort the initiative before it had a chance to prove itself.[56]

Without limitations on offensive arms this Administration may be reduced to arguing, as the Nixon Administration was forced to when promoting the *Safeguard* ABM system fifteen years ago, that the Soviet Union will maintain sufficient offensive forces to warrant making the effort but would not build them up to a level that would overwhelm the defence.

The offence–defence duel is not about to swing in favour of the defence, and the effectiveness of strategic defences in the future will depend as much on offensive constraints as on technological innovations. This leads to the proposition that the primary objectives informing the SDI might be more readily achieved by negotiated offensive limitations. Disarmament is certainly cheaper than strategic defence, it could begin right away, and the margins of error with regard to verification might well be far less than the potential leakage in a high-technology defensive system. It would also be under human control and not depend on a highly complex system to perform exactly to specification at its first serious test in the moments after a Soviet missile launch (or what might be suspected to be a Soviet missile launch) – and while the President is still being alerted to the fact that something may be happening.

Consider the consequences of a failure of a multilayered defence to perform as advertized. If, as a result of the deployment of this defence, the enemy had increased its offensive capabilities in order to deal with expected performance levels which were *not* reached at the critical moment, the result would be that far more warheads than would otherwise be the case would land on the homeland. The system would have been utterly counterproductive.

If the President really wants to eliminate offensive nuclear weapons from the face of the earth, why not propose just that to the Soviet Union? If it is desired to reduce the target sets available to the nuclear offensive, then reduce the flexibility by cutting its numbers. If it is desired to limit the damage to the United States should deterrence fail and reduce the risk of the nuclear winter, then at the very least propose reductions to small stockpiles.

There are of course objections to all these proposals but the issues of principle raised are no different from those connected with the SDI, and the practical difficulties, while significant, are nothing as compared with the introduction of effective strategic defences.

Conclusion
One major difference between disarmament and the Strategic Defense Initiative is that, whereas the former requires early and active co-operation between the United States and the Soviet Union, with the latter there is only a presumption that the two will follow a similar path because of similar calculations as to their security interests. This may lead some to hope that if only the United States can identify her interests more clearly, inherent economic and technical strengths will see her through to a decisive strategic breakthrough.

There is an ambiguity running through the whole SDI. Is this designed to restructure the super-power relationship on a quite different but still essentially equal basis? Or is it a unilateral strategic move by the United States to achieve an advantage over the Soviet Union?

In the more recent promotion of the SDI, considerable stress has been put on the risk of the USSR winning this new strategic race. Thus Lt-General Abrahamson has stated:

Were they [the Russians] to deploy the fruits of their programs unilaterally, the consequences to our national security would be grave.[57]

Why would it be grave? Possibly for the same reasons that the Soviet Union might believe it to be grave if the United States got there first. Whatever the protestations of peaceful intent and in the absence of negotiated constraints, a strategic defence is only likely to be most effective if the other side's offence has already been depleted through a first strike – the logical first layer of a multilayered defence.

In his original speech the President remarked:

I clearly recognise that defensive systems have limitations and raise certain problems and ambiguities. If paired with offensive systems, they can be viewed as fostering an aggressive policy and no one wants that.

It is now clear that, with the revision of the SDI away from the President's original utopianism, defensive and offensive systems are likely to be paired. What seems at times to be envisaged is not so much a tidy substitution of the defence for the offence but a continuing competition across the board in offensive and defensive systems, with strategists on both sides exploring areas of comparative advantage. It appears to be part of the continuing effort to develop plans for a nuclear strategy that is similar to conventional strategy in its flexibility and control.

The problems that have already been identified in conducting a controlled nuclear war in today's relatively straightforward strategic environment would be as nothing compared with the more confused environment now envisaged. A President is even less likely to be confronted with a credible war plan in this environment. Meanwhile the problems of crisis management would intensify. There would be doubts as to whether one's own defences were functioning properly combined with fears that the other's were completely reliable, and uncertainties over what sort of interference with the other side's defences would be sufficiently provocative to trigger war. And still there, at the back of everybody's minds, would be the sure knowledge that if things got out of hand, and who could say that they would not, the end result could be mutual destruction.

President Reagan's speech of March 1983 may have launched a thousand research projects but it did not launch a strategic revolution. He was offering a false prospect of invulnerability, an illusion that he had some bold escape plan from the harsh realities of the nuclear age. This would have quickly been dismissed as the ramblings of a senti-mental idealist had he not been President of the United States and had he not backed up his vision with the promise of a technical solution that was soon found to be wanting.

As dreams go, this one did not last long – about six months. But as the dream was forgotten the initiative that it had inspired rolled slowly into motion, imbued with a contrived sense of scientific adventure and still masquerading as a strategic revolution. So far the resources devoted to this enterprise have not been large but they could become substantial. Other costs will still be incurred. This episode has done little for the President's reputation as a responsible leader, has put additional strain on arms control and inserted another controversy into the Alliance. Most seriously of all it has served as yet another distraction for those unwilling to face up to real dilemmas that confront us in the strategic environment of the mid-1980s.

NOTES

[1] President Ronald Reagan, Speech on 'Defense Spending and Defensive Technology', 23 March 1983.

[2] My method in this Paper has been to rely throughout on statements from Administration sources. Using no more than these sources it is possible to establish a vigorous debate on the objectives, scope and prospects of the SDI.

[3] David Alan Rosenberg, 'The Origins of Overkill: Nuclear Weapons and American Strategy, 1945–1960', International Security, Spring 1983, p. 32.

[4] Secretary of Defense James Schlesinger, *Annual Defense Department Report FY 1975*, 4 March 1974, p. 67.

[5] One of the most effective who also put great stress on the potential of ABM technology was Don Brennan. See, for example, his 'The Case for Population Defense', in Johan Holst and William Schneider (eds), *Why ABM? Policy Issues in the Missile Defense Controversy* (New York: Pergamon Press, 1969).

[6] For a representative sample of views on the ABM issue in the early 1980s see 'ABM Revisited: Promise or Peril?', *Washington Quarterly*, Fall 1981.

[7] Strategic defence as a necessary alternative to assured destruction has been a constant theme of the Administration's case since March 1983, despite the fact that previous policies which had not involved BMD (and which did not require 25 years to yield fruit) were already supposed to have brought the 'MAD era' to a close. For an early presentation of the policy along these lines, see Fred Ikle 'The Vision vs The Nightmare', *Washington Post*, 27 March 1983.

[8] *Report of the President's Commission on Strategic Forces* (Washington DC: USGPO April 1983), pp. 9, 12.

[9] *President's Statement, 22 November 1982, Current Policy, No. 435* (Washington DC: Department of State, November 1982). This was the statement that announced the MX *Densepack* basing mode.

[10] 'We continue treaty-permitted R&D on Ballistic Missile Defense as a hedge against Soviet breakthroughs or breakouts that could threaten our retaliatory capability, and as a possible point defense option to enhance the survivability of our ICBM force', Secretary of Defense Harold Brown, *Department of Defense Annual Report, Fiscal Year 1982* (Washington DC: USGPO, 19 January 1981), p. 116.

[11] According to *Time*, 4 April 1983, the President discussed the issue with Keyworth in 1981. Keyworth set up an advisory group including Edward Teller, Consultant Edward Frieman and Former Deputy Secretary of Defense David Packard to study ABM and they reported early in 1983 that the idea seemed technically feasible. It was brought up briefly at a National Security Council meeting on 11 February 1983 after which nothing happened until the President himself raised the issue with National Security Adviser William Clark. The Pentagon and the State Department were to study the problem further (but not ACDA). However, the President decided that he would prefer to announce the plan with some fanfare rather than let it be studied quietly.

[12] Press Conference, quoted in *New York Times*, 26 March 1983.

[13] *NBC*, 'Meet the Press', 27 March 1983 (Quoted in *Baltimore Sun*, 28 March 1983). See also the report of the news conference of 24 March (*New York Times*, 25 March 1983). However, it is of note that Keyworth was more relaxed on this score. 'The objective is to have a system that would convince an adversary that an offensive attack will not be successful. It has to be a very effec-

tive system, but it would not have to be perfect to convince an adversary that his attack would fail'. Interview, *US News & World Report*, 11 April 1983.

14 The briefing accompanying the President's speech confirmed that he was not talking about bombers or cruise missiles, *Aerospace Daily*, 29 March 1983. On the rationale see Weinberger quoted in *Government Executive*, July/August 1983.

15 Reagan Press Conference, 29 March 1983; Weinberger 'Meet the Press', 27 March 1983.

16 Speech to National Press Club, Washington DC, quoted in *Baltimore Sun*, 2 May 1984. The shift is clearly illustrated by two quotations from George Keyworth, a year apart. In June 1983 he told an interviewer that: 'It may be a worthwhile technological development to defend your offensive missile capability, but it is only marginal to the President's overall strategic objective, which is to move from a dependence on offense to a dependence on defense', *C&EN*, 20 June 1983. In June 1984 he told an audience in Dallas that the President had a near-term as well as a long-term goal. The initial goal was to protect only the US strategic missiles through a primitive capability to intercept ICBM during the boost phase, *Washington Post*, 17 June 1984. However, Keyworth remains true to the ultimate objective. See, for example, his 'A Sense of Obligation: The Strategic Defense Initiative', *Aerospace America*, April 1984. See also *National Journal*, 17 March 1984.

17 *New York Times*, 10 May 1984.

18 For example Robert Jastrow: 'Reagan vs the Scientists: Why the President is Right about Missile Defense', *Commentary*, January 1984. 'Critics of President Reagan's plan spoke as if he were proposing a defense of entire cities and their populations, but he made no such suggestion of that kind in his speech'.

19 *Aviation Week & Space Technology*, 24 October 1984. Summaries of all three reports can be found in *Senate Foreign Relations Committee, Strategic Defense and Anti-Satellite Weapons* (25 April 1984).

20 The Republican Platform for the 1984 elections stated that in order to 'begin to eliminate' the nuclear missile threat, 'we will use superior American technology to achieve space-based and ground-based defensive systems as soon as possible'. A White House aide was reported to have complained that this statement was 'a little more futuristic than we would have wanted it', but claimed that it had been toned down by substituting 'achieve' for 'build', *Baltimore Sun*, 23 August 1984.

21 *Washington Post*, 26 January 1984.

22 For example Charles Mohr in *New York Times*, 23 March 1984, quotes Richard De Lauer, Under Secretary of Defense for Research and Engineering, informing Congress that 'Our state of knowledge of the relevant technologies is inadequate' and that an 'informed decision on whether to go ahead with a system could not be taken until the early 1990s', and Robert S. Cooper, Director of the Defense Advance Research Projects Agency, admitted that the researchers had no 'gold, silver or platinum bullet' in sight against missiles. See also *Washington Post*, 24 March 1984.

23 *Washington Post*, 25 August 1984. George Keyworth has specifically linked the SDI with 'capabilities to defend more effectively against the air-breathing threat of air-

planes and cruise missiles'. Lt-General Abrahamson, however, has stated that: 'At this time in the program there is clearly no (such) mandate', *Science*, 10 August 1984.

24 Lt-General James Abrahamson, *Testimony to the Defense Subcommittee of the House Appropriations Committee* (11 May 1984). Richard Cooper, Director of DARPA told the Senate Foreign Relations Committee (26 April 1984): 'If we decided say in 1995 or the year 2000 to do this it would take us 10–20 years to put it in place'.

25 Prior to the President's speech some $1 bn was being spent on strategic defence. This was expected to grow by about $500 m in FY 1984 without the new initiative, which in fact added only some $250 m of new funding. After Congressional cuts the level of funding was not far off its previous target (although the balance of spending has been substantially altered, with a shift away from the preparation of a system capable of early development to the investigation of the more exotic technologies. According to a Congressional Budget Office study, prior to the new initiative less than 30% went on new technologies; that proportion has now jumped to 55%, *Washington Times*, 24 May 1984.) For FY 1985 some $3.8 bn is being requested, and during FY 1986–9 some $25 bn is required. It has been reported that two-thirds of this amount ($15–18 bn) might have been spent even without the new initiative, *Baltimore Sun*, 13 May 1984.

26 *Hearings before the Research and Development and Investigations Subcommittees of the House Committee on Armed Services, HR 3073 People Protection Act* (10 November 1983), p. 26. In 1981 the cost of a damage denial system was put by Administration witnesses to a subcommittee of the Senate Armed Services at a figure of $500 bn, with a limited defence costing some $100 bn, *New York Times*, 31 March 1983.

27 On the difficulties of getting the Pentagon and Congress interested in a $7.5 bn plan to improve US air defences see *Wall Street Journal*, 28 March 1984.

28 See, for example, General T. R. Milton USAF (Ret.), 'Talking Real Money', *Air Force Magazine*, July 1984.

29 *Science*, 10 August 1984.

30 The intermediate rationale is developed in Fred S. Hoffman, *Ballistic Missile Defense and US National Security, Summary Report*, prepared for Future Security Strategy Study (October 1983) and in Keith Payne and Colin Gray, 'Nuclear Policy and the Defensive Transition', *Foreign Affairs*, Spring 1984.

31 Payne and Gray, *ibid.*, p. 840.

32 Defense Department General Counsel William H. Taft IV challenged the 'Congressional Findings' section of the proposed People Protection Act which stated that that 'The President has called for changes in United States strategic policy that seek to save lives in time of war', on the grounds that the objective was to reduce the 'likelihood of war'. Quoted in Ashton Carter, *Directed Energy Missile Defense in Space* (Washington DC: Congress of the United States, Office of Technology Assessment, April 1984), p. 65.

33 A 'national campaign to save the ABM Treaty' is reported to favour research on advanced ABM systems as a hedge against a Soviet break-out, *Washington Post*, 20 June 1984.

[34] The late 1983 interagency report following up the President's speech is believed to have stated that: 'Even prior to deployment, the demonstration of US technology would strengthen military and negotiating stances'. Quoted in William Arkin, 'SDI – Pie in the Sky?', *Bulletin of Atomic Scientists*, April 1984.

[35] Thus we find the following in the interagency report: 'By constructing or eliminating the effectiveness of both limited and major attack options against key US military targets and thus leaving only options for attacking urban areas – which would be of highly questionable credibility – defences could significantly reduce the utility of strategic and theater nuclear forces and raise the threshold of nuclear conflict'. *Defense Against Ballistic Missiles: An Assessment of Technologies and Policy Implications* (Washington DC: DOD, March 1984). For those who suspect the opposite there is a precedent for this. In the early 1960s when the US adopted a 'cities-avoidance' strategy and backed this up with a surge in missile production the Soviet Union lacked a comparable capability and so was forced to stress the more terroristic aspects of her nuclear arsenal (for example by exploding a 56 megaton nuclear device).

[36] Speech delivered at University of Virginia, reproduced in *Science and Government Report*, 15 July 1984.

[37] *Baltimore Sun*, 24 April 1984; *Boston Globe*, 30 July 1984. On his return from Turkey, West German Defence Minister Manfred Wörner expressed his concern that the US programme should not 'open up a new dimension in the arms race', *International Herald Tribune*, 12 April 1984. More recently he has toned down his criticisms on the basis of assurances that the US is only seeking parity in research and development to the Soviet Union and that any eventual defensive protection would be extended to Europe, *Baltimore Sun*, 13 July 1984. Although in private the British have expressed worries, they have refrained from doing so publicly taking a 'wait and see' view. See, for example, the testimony of Defence Secretary Michael Heseltine to the House of Commons Select Committee on Defence, *Statement on the Defence Estimates 1984 First Report, Session 1983–84* (22 May 1984). For a discussion of the stakes of the British and French in the ABM Treaty, see Lawrence Freedman, 'The Small Nuclear Powers', in Ashton Carter and David Schwarz (eds), *Ballistic Missile Defense* (Washington DC: Brookings Institution, 1984).

[38] See Lawrence Freedman, 'Europe and the ABM Revival' in Ian Bellany and Coit Blacker (eds), *Antiballistic Missile Defence in the 1980s* (London: Frank Cass, 1983).

[39] Richard De Lauer told a Congressional Committee that: 'Included in the program are technologies for defense against the shorter range nuclear ballistic missiles . . . which may not have trajectories high enough to permit their attack with exoatmospheric systems, and which have short times-of-flight. Such technologies are important for defense of our allies'. *Statement before the Subcommittee on Research and Development of the Committee on Armed Services, House of Representatives* (1 March 1984). On *Patriot* as a TABM see *Aviation Week & Space Technology*, 9 April 1984; *International Herald Tribune*, 5 April 1984. The *Hawk* SAM is being considered as an anti-cruise missile weapon.

[40] *New York Times*, 18 July 1984.

[41] *Aerospace Daily*, 18 November 1983.

[42] Quoted in the *Washington Times*, 19 June 1984. The two most substantial critical studies are the report prepared by the Union of Concerned Scientists, *Space-based Missile Defense* (Cambridge, Mass.: March 1983) and Ashton B. Carter, *Directed Energy Missile Defense in Space* (Washington DC: Congress of the United States, Office of Technology Assessment, April 1984).

[43] In his speech the President acknowledged that the technology might not be ready for decades but said that 'current technology has now reached the point where it is reasonable for us to begin the effort'. A few hours earlier, Major-General Donald Lamberson, an assistant to Richard De Lauer, had been asked by a Senate subcommittee whether he could recommend 'an acceleration of the space-based laser technology program on technical grounds'. He answered 'Senator, no, I cannot at this point in time', quoted in *Washington Post*, 1 April 1984. Richard De Lauer himself was quoted as saying with regard to exotic ballistic missiles defenses that their difficulty has been 'understated', *New York Times*, 1 April 1984.

[44] For a report suggesting that many members of the Fletcher Commission are unhappy at the way that their report has been used to confirm the feasibility of SDI (rather than just to suggest that it deserved to be researched), see *National Journal*, 7 July 1984.

[45] Jastrow, *op. cit.* in note 18, p. 29.

[46] DOD Report (Washington DC: USGPO, March 1964). See note 36.

[47] See note 24.

[48] 'When they see that we have embarked on a long-term effort to achieve an extremely effective defense, supported by a strong national will, they will give up on the development of more offensive missiles and move in the same direction', *Science*, 10 August 1984. One of his principal scientific assistants, Gerold Vonas, has suggested that this effect will appear as soon as real technological achievements have been demonstrated: 'As the Soviets see these technology achievements they will begin to question the validity of their previous investment in strategic weapons'. *Aviation Week & Space Technology*, 8 October 1984.

[49] According to Soviet scientist E. P. Velikhov: 'Our country – relying on its powerful scientific, technological and economic potential – is quite capable of responding as appropriate. But we will take our own road', *Washington Post*, 24 June 1984. For an extremely useful discussion of the Soviet response, see Sidney D. Drell, Philip J. Farley and David Holloway, *The Reagan Strategic Defense Initiative: A Technical, Political, and Arms Control Assessment*, A Special report of the Center for International Security and Arms Control (Stanford Ca: Stanford UP, July 1984).

[50] According to Richard De Lauer, 'There's no way an enemy can't overwhelm your defenses if he wants to badly enough. It makes a lot of difference in what we do if we have to defend against 1000 RVs or 10,000', quoted in *Government Executive*, July/August 1983.

[51] James A. Thomson, *Strategic Defense and Deterrence, Statement before the Defense Appropriations Subcommittee of the House Appropriations Committee* (9 May 1984).

52 Dr James Fletcher, *Statement before the Sub-committee on Research and Development of the Committee on Armed Services, House of Representatives* (1 March 1984).

53 The Administration has charged that a Soviet radar under construction at Krasnoyarsk in Central Siberia, is 'almost certainly' a violation of Article VI, paragraph B of the ABM Treaty which states that 'future radars for early warning of strategic ballistic missile attack' should not be constructed 'except at locations along the periphery of its national territory oriented outward'. This radar is 500 miles back from the border and oriented towards the Siberian landmass. The Soviet Union has responded that this radar is for space tracking which is allowed under the Treaty. *The President's Report to the Congress on Soviet Noncompliance with Arms Control Agreements* (23 January 1984). The June 1984 HOE test using a *Minuteman*–I booster could be in contravention of Article VI(a) which, *inter alia*, precludes giving missiles other than ABM interceptor missiles capabilities to counter strategic ballistic missiles in their flight trajectory and testing them in an ABM mode. Testing of technologies suitable for ABM in an ASAT mode could also be considered to be in violation (see note 54).

54 George Keyworth is quoted as saying that: 'It may not necessarily be the best way for the ASAT mission but a geosynchronous anti-satellite capability is important to test the technology to destroy missiles', *Aviation Week & Space Technology*, 18 July 1983. The *Talon–Gold* spotting and tracking system which is relevant to both ASAT and SDI is another example of this link.

55 Strobe Talbot, *Deadly Gambits: The Reagan Administration and the Stalemate in Nuclear Arms Control* (New York: Alfred A. Knopf, 1984), p. 320.

56 'Most of the people in this Administration feel that you build the system before you do arms control. A completer ban on weapons in space would tend to foreclose most of your most effective strategic defense options'. Major Peter Worden, quoted in *Science*, 10 August 1984.

57 *Aviation Week & Space Technology*, 21 May 1984. There is little doubt that the Soviet Union has been engaged in active research in the relevant areas. According to Richard De Lauer, the two sides are equal in laser technology, the Soviet Union is ahead in large rockets able to lift heavy loads in space and the United States is ahead in data processing. What is interesting is that heavy boosters is one of those areas where the Fletcher Commission recommended putting off research because it would be relatively easy to catch up if progress was made in the more difficult areas. On the other hand, data processing has been acknowledged to be the most critical area for the success of any SDI.

Conclusions

DR ROBERT O'NEILL

Our opening plenary Papers, in setting the stage for the committee discussions, led our thoughts through closely interconnected issues. Although they did not trespass greatly on each other's vital ground, each author showed that the future of his field would be influenced by developments in the others. The credibility and stability of deterrence rests on both nuclear and conventional forces, as well as on arms-control measures. It rests also, as the French Foreign Minister Cheysson (in his opening remarks) and Ambassador Abshire reminded us, on the interplay of national and international politics. M. Cheysson gave us timely advice that we need to address all of these factors if we are to produce something useful to national and Alliance leaders.

Each of the authors of these opening plenary Papers judged technology to be at least neutral, although Henri Conze warned us particularly to beware of deluding ourselves that it can, in the short term, change the East–West balance, or that new conventional technologies can greatly reduce our dependence on nuclear weapons. In other words we should put ourselves, and our leaders, in the dock rather than technology itself or those who foster it.

Technology and Strategic Systems

Clearly, technological developments pose many problems for the continued viability of strategic systems, old and new. Brent Scowcroft drew our attention to several of them: increasing missile accuracy; decreasing ICBM survivability; increasing vulnerability of C^3 systems; decreasing survivability and penetration powers of bombers; possible breakthroughs in strategic ASW; the double-edged nature of the sea-launched cruise missile; and the problems of ballistic missile defences.

Many of these concerns were reflected in the discussion of Committees 1 and 2 (on the Strategic Defense Initiative (SDI) debate and land-based systems). The debate in Committee 1 was characterized as 'surprisingly rational', leading some to feel, probably wrongly, that significant consensus emerged. Others noted that it concealed deep passions deriving from differing perceptions of the world and Alliance policies, passions which for the most part were kept in check but on occasion burst forth to remind us that this was a debate of no mean or transient significance.

The technical feasibility of the whole concept came under strong challenge but Fred Hoffman offered a stout defence of the decision to carry out more research in this area. There was wide agreement with Lawrence Freedman that the technical problems to be overcome were daunting although David Schwartz, in accord with a theme which was common to most committee discussions, cautioned that it is difficult to judge a project so enveloped in uncertainty regarding cost and its effect on Soviet–American relations, arms control and extended deterrence.

Debate moved to the question of whether Mutual Assured Destruction (MAD) could or should be set aside by ballistic missile defence (BMD). Some, in support of the SDI, contended that the Soviet Union did not accept MAD and that MAD in any event neutralized the possibility of limited Western nuclear responses to Soviet aggression. Others, opposed to the SDI, pointed out that whether or not the Soviet Union accepted MAD as a doctrine, it was a fact and they had to take it into account in calculating consequences of any move against the West. Similarly the West had to accept it, unless a highly leak-proof system of defence could be developed which took care not only of ballistic missiles but also aircraft, cruise missiles and all other means of nuclear delivery against cities.

Proponents of BMD responded that it did not have to be leak-proof to be useful, particularly through its capacity to complicate Soviet planning for attack on military targets. Defences would improve deterrence, frustrating both limited and full-scale attacks. Opponents stressed that any system that was not leak-proof left cities vulnerable and popular support for it would be difficult to win. What would be the worth of such a huge and costly effort? What would be the opportunity costs?

Soviet responses to the SDI in terms of offensive force structure were also disputed, some arguing that it would impel them to negotiate lower agreed limits but many more contending that offensive force increases, together with more re-entry vehicles and penetration aids, would be the result. The likely Soviet defensive response was not as contested an issue, although opinions varied on how seriously the Soviet Union was already committed to a BMD programme of her own. A significant Soviet BMD capability would inhibit Western nuclear options, particularly important for extended deterrence. The West stands in greater need of such options than the Soviet Union.

At the end of the debate, there was general agreement on the desirability of pursuit of some BMD research as a prudent hedge against Soviet breakout, although Richard Garwin declared that a more effective option would be to counter Soviet BMD with better US penetration aids. This view was contested by Albert Wohlstetter. But many, particularly Europeans, saw the full SDI programme as very divisive within the Alliance, placing a strain where it was not needed, and risking the undoing of many years of promoting a sense of solidarity of shared risks. Albert Carnesale summed up the European argument thus: 'Western Europe objects to any change in a security system that seems to be working well enough as it is; therefore the burden of proof is on those who propose change'.

In terms of the effect of the SDI on arms control, those supporting the proposal argued that it could provide leverage to bring the Soviet Union back to strategic negotiations and, conversely, that arms-control agreements to limit offensive forces would strengthen the effectiveness of BMD. Opponents argued that BMD would work in the opposite direction, leading to offensive force increases and, most particularly, abrogation of the ABM Treaty which would open the door to the development of high altitude anti-satellite (ASAT) devices and cause widespread popular dissent in the West, notably Europe. Clearly the Reagan Administration has a long way to go in terms of convincing informed Westerners that the SDI is a wise move, and efforts to do so will once again cause severe Alliance strains.

Committee 2, in reviewing the future of land-based strategic systems, agreed that some such weapons would be essential to the West for a long time to come, despite their increasing vulnerability. They could be replaced in part by other systems such as the D-5 SLBM but for reasons of command and control, battle management and maintaining secrecy of SSBN deployments, ICBM should be retained. Some participants, particularly from the host country (France), pointed to the difference between having missiles on one's own soil and having them at sea, in terms of the greater psychological and political impact of an enemy strike on home territory compared with loss of a submarine at sea.

Survivability was clearly the major problem to be solved and, in view of the increasing accuracy of Soviet missiles, mobility seemed to offer more hope than super-hardening of silos. It also had to be remembered that all strategic systems were vulnerable, albeit to differing degrees, and the true art of force structure was to build, out of individually vulnerable elements, a total deterrent whose viability as an entire force could not be questioned in any remotely probable circumstances. Nonetheless, severe political and fiscal problems currently block the way towards deployment of a new US ICBM system and the operational doubts already raised about proposed new systems and basing modes are formidable.

The Soviet Union could be expected to continue to place great reliance on land-based systems. Her geographic situation and political structure greatly eased the difficulties of their deployments. Her new missiles under development were impressive and there was seen to be no likelihood that the US would wish to follow suit to that degree. The future for ICBM is thus somewhat unbalanced between East and West and there is little prospect of it changing. French participants emphasized the continuing important role that their land-based strategic missiles would play. Some Americans argued that fewer and more vulnerable ICBM still represented a wise investment, provided that there was approximate equivalence with the USSR in all three legs of the Triad.

Nonetheless, such matters were held by others to be purely academic because of the political difficulties in the way of any mooted US deployment. The debate on this whole question was thus strongly political rather than narrowly strategic.

Conventional Technologies

As if the problems of strategic systems were not bad enough, Henri Conze threw some iced water on those who hope for a drastic improvement in the conventional balance through a technological revolution. It is salutary for us to note, given his professional experience, his scepticism about the importance of new technologies. This attitude undercuts to some extent his concern that the debate on this topic might postpone the taking of real action, but it does not remove it. The urgency of improving the conventional defences of the West gives us little choice but to act, but we must do so carefully and selectively. What Conze, between the lines, and other participants not so indirectly, have told us is that improvement must come through progress on many fronts: manpower; individual training and motivation; tactical proficiency; and organization. Where technology can help most, Conze advises us, is in target acquisition and recognition, electronic warfare, C³, and new materials for missiles, engines, armour and enhanced computing power.

In assessing the impact of new technology on the NATO–Warsaw Pact balance, the committee discussions focused on several topics, but perhaps most interestingly on the relationship between technology and opera-

tional concepts. These discussions were predicated on awareness that great uncertainties attend any assessment of the impact of new technologies. We have little idea as to how rapidly they are likely to be deployed on either side. Cost estimates may be wildly wrong. The money required may bite into other areas of defence preparedness in ways that are difficult to anticipate. The systems are of such complexity that their operational use may be restricted, requiring the maintenance of existing systems to close the gaps in coverage.

Despite these uncertainties, nobody disputed that new technologies would come into wide use and impact strongly on operational capabilities and doctrines. But there was hot debate on whether or not the Soviet Union would adapt her own doctrines to reduce significantly the vulnerability of her forces to such new Western capabilities. This discussion revealed significant divergence of view as to what Soviet doctrines actually are, with some believing that Operational Manoeuvre Groups (OMG) have a more modest probing function while others contended that their role is more strategic and extensive. In any event, a growing Western capability to strike targets, fixed or mobile, at considerably greater range than today, would induce Soviet leaders to avoid major force concentrations until the very last moment, thereby complicating their planning. We need to do further work on the implications of this vulnerability for the OMG concept as a whole before we can conclude the arguments as to whether the costs of new technology equipment programmes are justified. The intensity of this debate and the fundamental nature of the topic suggest that we should increase our efforts to probe these doctrinal questions.

Until these doubts are resolved it is very difficult to assess the worth of the Follow-On Forces Attack (FOFA) concept to the point that trade-off evaluations can be made with any accuracy. Hence the development of new-technology forces to implement FOFA operations may be misdirected or considerably delayed. Critics also pointed to the dangers inherent in the FOFA concept of reliance on a wide array of real-time command, control and data processing facilities. Such responsiveness may well prove unattainable under operational conditions, thereby nullifying the worth of major investments which will have depleted alternate means of operating.

These doubts were countered by 'emerging technologies' (ET) advocates who argued that the debate should not be only about FOFA because there were many other missions that new technologies would facilitate. They also challenged their opponents to produce better proposals and pointed to the importance of ET in raising the nuclear threshold. Of course it can be argued that what in fact raises the nuclear threshold is NATO's reluctance to be the first to use nuclear weapons because of the Soviet attainment of nuclear parity, rather than enhanced Western conventional capability. Nonetheless there seemed to be wide agreement, particularly amongst Europeans, that new technologies had a vital role to play in closing the conventional gap and that public opinion would support new investments, particularly in developing capabilities that strengthen defence on and around the Central Front itself rather than against forces coming from a long way behind it.

Thus, while public controversy builds up on the 'deep strike' issues, there is a good prospect that public confidence in Western defence concepts may be regenerated by judicious procurement of equipment designed to increase greatly the losses of enemy forces within 40 kilometres of the front line, to quote one of the participants who seemed to be the least common denominator of the group. Others thought that public opinion would support considerable deepening of the target area.

Concern was expressed also about the difficulties of maintaining political control of operations in the new technology environment. Some argued that the speed of operations would inhibit political leaders from using their real-time C³I capabilities to the full, giving the military freer rein than before. Sir Harry Tuzo pointed to the way in which use of new technology systems could border on pre-emption, requiring extremely strict political controls in time of tension before any outbreak of hostilities.

Out of these discussions came awareness of a need for more analysis of criteria for determining the mix of nuclear and conventional forces, investigation of the above-mentioned uncertainties involved in new-technology force development, and study of the likely Soviet responses to various NATO policies.

In the light of all these uncertainties, the difficulties inherent in the task of Committee 4, on implications for force structure and rationalization, are not difficult to comprehend. Yet it moved in a thorough and workmanlike way to investigate the constraints on such developments and ways of overcoming them. The constraints identified included: the conservative effect of existing force structures; differences in interpretation of what Flexible Response actually means (and hence how to fashion forces for that strategy); general economic pressures; unwillingness of European governments to yield up any of their sovereignty; and the political dilemmas created by new technology concepts, particularly for the Federal Republic of Germany, in attempting to improve relations with the East while at the same time reinforcing capabilities to retaliate in depth against Warsaw Pact forces.

Although lengthy discussion of a transatlantic division of labour failed to produce coherent results, other than to reject Senator Nunn's hope that Europeans might provide their own defence against a first echelon attack while the United States would reinforce against a second, the need for such a division of labour was clear.

As a general mechanism the United States should encourage the formation of European consortia to produce the new equipment that will be required, turning what has been described as 'a one way autobahn and thirteen footpaths' into something more like a two-way street.

Economic constraints dictated the assertion of a strict order of procurement priorities for the major new equipment and stock-building that is needed. Such priorities had to be agreed on an Alliance-wide basis and the task was seen as urgent.

Little, if any, progress seems to have been made in the area of rationalization scouted in Ingemar Dörfer's paper. His emphasis on the utility of spending more on reserve forces is worth noting, although the means of payment, namely funds currently earmarked for European air force modernization to be released by the stationing of six more US air wings in Europe, are unlikely to be realised. Nevertheless, rationalization in less spectacular areas may prove possible and is certainly desirable if Europe is to achieve a defence strength fully comparable with its economic and demographic resources.

Implications for Arms Control

In introducing our discussion on the implications of new technologies for arms control, Walt Slocombe argued against the mood of despair which so often accompanies such debate. While appreciating the way in which technological change *can* undermine the utility of existing agreements, he pointed out in his treatment of BMD that it *need* not, and indeed could serve as a reinforcement for the ABM Treaty. However, given the Soviet proclivity to press to the limits of compliance and beyond, as in the case of the Pushkino phased-array radar, a little technological leverage may well prove essential for the US. The implications of the SDI in this regard may not be so helpful, however, particularly if the Soviet Union interprets the planned research programme as an indication that the US intends to break the ABM Treaty.

In accepting the desirability of land mobility as the best solution to the problem of ICBM vulnerability, Slocombe warns that methods for deployment must be part of future arms-control agreements. Hence this factor must be taken into account now in designing deployment options. On satellite vulnerability he draws our attention to the possibilities of a ban on high-altitude ASAT tests and limits on space- or ground-based laser and other directed-energy ASAT devices. He recognizes the dual-capability problem as serious but gives us hope that technology can help effective verification rather than frustrate it.

In the prevailing political climate it is difficult to see much, if any, of this agenda being carried into practice. Indeed one cannot help but be struck by a general atmosphere of hopelessness regarding the short-term future

of arms control, both within this conference and amongst the wider professional community. One hopes that some will respond by generating new approaches but we are forced to recognize that until there is a change in the climate of East–West relations, the incentives to do so are few.

Pierre Lellouche highlighted the close linkages which this situation encourages between technology, strategic doctrine and arms control. Technological change or uncertainty raises questions both for our doctrines and our arms-control policies. At a time when the potential for change in doctrines is high, we must also expect change in our arms-control policies. Until we have settled our doctrines, we will not be able to settle our arms-control policies.

In view of the difficulties encountered by the committees in discussing doctrines, it is not surprising therefore that the arms-control committee found it hard to propose new steps which had any prospect of achievement. Much of its discussion focused on the causes of the current deadlock, which were perceived as being essentially political, with particular reference made to underdeveloped awareness of security interdependence by both sides. The committee supported Walt Slocombe's view that, although technology caused complications for arms control, it was not responsible for the current impasse. The idea that technology, once discovered, somehow pushed its way into weapons deployments while nobody was watching was rejected. The outlook, not surprisingly, is pessimistic: the causes of the deadlock were agreed as long-lasting. Even should the political climate moderate in 1985, years would be required for it to find expression in new arms-control agreements. These East–West tensions are bound to feed West–West strains, although the Soviet Union seems reliable in terms of saving us from total disarray by her own ill-calculated behaviour. Should she ever become adroit in long-term diplomacy we will really be in trouble.

Despite this chilly prospect, the committee discussions evinced considerable enthusiasm for at least attempting a new round of negotiations emphasizing ASAT controls. Other means believed to be worth further investigation were a chemical warfare (CW) treaty and, unilaterally, ways of controlling testing and improving verification techniques. The notion of preventive or pre-emptive arms control did not attract much support. Some agreed that problems such as BMD would provide an incentive for both sides to return to negotiations to limit offensive weapons. Many others countered that the logic is more likely to run in the reverse direction.

The inter-relationship between technology, doctrine and arms control was seen as an important topic, but clearly it is insufficiently understood and stands before us as a challenge for future investigation. The conflictual relationship of deterrence does not sit easily alongside the co-operative relationship of arms control, yet indisputably there is an interaction between them which is intensified by technological change. Whether the quest to intensify changes which might assist both relationships together proves to be a search for the philosopher's stone remains to be seen. At least we can come to grips with the questions of trade-offs regarding those changes which either assist the one and impede other, or simply complicate both.

Technology Management in the Alliance
Problems of research and development policy were an even more important part of the work of Committee 5. In its discussion, heed was taken of the formidable political, economic, social and even, although somewhat ambiguously, military pressures which exist to maintain independent national R&D and production capabilities. Despite the acknowledged advantages of international specialization, most countries, particularly the larger states of Western Europe, remain understandably very reluctant to surrender capabilities before grim necessity forces them to do so. Increasing dependence on the US causes a wide array of problems in Europe, but willingness to pool resources effectively while good markets still exist for national European industries is low.

A comprehensive research and development effort could clearly influence beneficially industrial policies and industrial development, and there was recognition that shared R&D was highly desirable. History

over the past decades has demonstrated, however, that national or competitive elements intrude and make progress in this area difficult or impossible to achieve. Progress was relatively easier at the research, rather than the development stage. Shared research could be achieved as the recent efforts by Admiral Inman in America attest. One concrete suggestion to surmount some of the technical obstacles would be to concentrate Alliance research on some single technical production problem, such as production of higher-capacity microchips, since the proprietary aspects of such chips came not with the chips themselves but through the programmes, i.e., the 'software', applied to them. Techniques such as that might permit more across-the-board collaboration in later development.

Ambassador Abshire offers a prescription for a resources strategy designed to maximize gains from the limited capabilities of individual Alliance members. He points rightly to NATO's superior resources *vis-à-vis* the Warsaw Pact and its inferior record in military production. One does not need to go all the way with his analysis that the prime challenge to NATO in its second thirty-five years is resource management to acknowledge that this challenge is indeed in the first four or five. Alliance resource management needs to be founded on a better common military appreciation of the threat and a fuller conceptual or doctrinal framework. There is room for more co-ordinated guidance for national defence decisions which relate to Alliance needs, although it may not always be heeded. Special bodies for managing technological change such as the Conference of National Armaments Directors (CNAD) and the Independent European Programme Group (IEPG) should be strengthened and, to foster the growth of research and development investment in Europe, the notion of a European Advanced Research Agency is worth support. As Ambassador Abshire indicates, creation of organizations is not enough: political support is vital and it must rest on firm domestic and external foundations. As Committee 5's discussions suggest, much remains to be done to consolidate these foundations before any major new structure can be built.

56

Conclusion

Finally let me make a few general observations based on the experience of sitting in the plenaries and the committees, de-briefing the rapporteurs and thinking about their reports. New technology is coming, as surely as day follows night; and coming on a wide front. Individual developments may not be as revolutionary as were nuclear weapons, but major changes are coming in many, many areas and their management and absorption pose major challenges. There will be delays and bottlenecks. It will happen by gradual increments, like a slowly breaking wave, whose overall impact is nonetheless tremendous. Behind this wave are more. Some we will catch; some we will miss. It is no use complaining: if we want to live in our present style and standard, we have to learn to manage change.

The waves seem likely to continue to be slow, but if they are too slow we will be becalmed. We need to maintain and stimulate their creative energy. The new technology will be expensive. It can easily prove too expensive if not properly managed. Yet, given the political, social and demographic differences between the Soviet Union and the West, we need it to be sure of our security. Furthermore, we are not blind to the advances in military technology made by the Soviet Union, although we are also aware that they are not moving so fast and so effectively that their policies cannot be affected by our own pace of development.

In all this haste, we must not sacrifice military effectiveness and stability simply in order to take on new devices. The Soviet leaders, as tough-minded, practical people are most unlikely to fall into this trap. We, with our greater pressures to accommodate to change, must remember that we face risks as well as gains and must learn to distinguish folly from enterprise.

Most of the committee discussions were, as their participants recognized, founded on uncertainty. It is hardly to be wondered at that they had difficulty in reaching specific conclusions. They bring home to us the awareness that in this environment of extensive technological change, uncertainty is pervasive – in technological capability, in strategic doctrine, in arms control, in political relations within the Alliance as well as with the Soviet Union. It is not going to fade, particularly in an age when major wars are not available as a laboratory for testing equipment, men and concepts. We must learn to live with it better than the Soviet Union. We ought to be able to, unless of course we are creating much more uncertainty in our own national houses than they are in theirs.

These remarks are written as a conclusion to the conference already held. In many ways they are also an introduction to the conference the Institute is planning for 1985. The IISS is not going to give up the search for a deeper understanding of the doctrines of East and West; and of how they relate to each other and to arms control under the influence of technological change. We will not repeat ourselves: we will go forward from this basis, however uncertain it might be. We will grapple with some of the bigger questions which this conference has opened up but, for good reasons, has been unable to close.

Nobody is flattered to be compared with Czar Nicholas II, of whose Hague Peace Conference of 1899 Michael Howard has written in the most recent issue of *International Security*, that it 'was no more than a ripple in the current of international politics'. Yet, if this conference in Avignon should achieve that status, we may feel well pleased.

RAYMOND H. FOGLER LIBRARY

DATE DUE

BOOKS ARE SUBJECT TO
RECALL AFTER TWO WEEKS

DEC 3 1 1987

FEB 2   1987

ADELPHI PAPERS

The following is a selection of those available. They may be ordered from the Institute at a current price of **£3.50**
($6.50), *post free (by Accelerated Surface Post or Bulk Air Mail to non-UK destinations).*

No. 168.   NUCLEAR WEAPONS IN EUROPE by Gregory Treverton. Summer 1981.
No. 169.   CAN NUCLEAR WAR BE CONTROLLED? by Desmond Ball. Autumn 1981.
No. 170.   GERMANY AND THE WESTERN ALLIANCE: LESSONS FROM THE 1980 CRISES by Philip Windsor. Autumn
            1981.
No. 171.   THE SPREAD OF NUCLEAR WEAPONS: MORE MAY BE BETTER by Kenneth N. Waltz. Autumn 1981.
No. 172.   CHINA AND SOUTH-EAST ASIA: STRATEGIC INTERESTS AND POLICY PROSPECTS by Takashi Tajima.
            Winter 1981.
No. 173.   AMERICA'S SECURITY IN THE 1980s: PART I: Papers from the IISS 23rd Annual Conference. Spring 1982.
No. 174.   AMERICA'S SECURITY IN THE 1980s: PART II: Papers from the IISS 23rd Annual Conference. Spring 1982.
No. 175.   DETERRENCE IN THE 1980s PART I: AMERICAN STRATEGIC FORCES AND EXTENDED DETERRENCE by
            Anthony H. Cordesman. Summer 1982.
No. 176.   MBFR: LESSONS AND PROBLEMS by Lothar Ruehl. Summer 1982.
No. 177.   ARMS CONTROL AND THE POLITICS OF EUROPEAN SECURITY by Theodor H. Winkler. Autumn 1982.
No. 178.   THE EVOLUTION OF JAPANESE SECURITY POLICY by Yukio Satoh. Autumn 1982.
No. 179.   GREEK SECURITY: ISSUES AND POLITICS by Thanos Veremis. Winter 1982.
No. 180.   A REGIONAL SECURITY ROLE FOR AFRICA'S FRONT-LINE STATES: EXPERIENCE AND PROSPECTS by
            Robert S. Jaster. Spring 1983.
No. 181.   NORDIC SECURITY by Erling Bjøl. Spring 1983.
No. 182.   DEFENCE AND CONSENSUS: THE DOMESTIC ASPECTS OF WESTERN SECURITY: PART I: Papers from the
            IISS 24th Annual Conference. Summer 1983.
No. 183.   DEFENCE AND CONSENSUS: THE DOMESTIC ASPECTS OF WESTERN SECURITY: PART II: Papers from the
            IISS 24th Annual Conference. Summer 1983.
No. 184.   DEFENCE AND CONSENSUS: THE DOMESTIC ASPECTS OF WESTERN SECURITY: PART III: Papers from the
            IISS 24th Annual Conference. Summer 1983.
No. 185.   TARGETING FOR STRATEGIC DETERRENCE by Desmond Ball. Summer 1983.
No. 186.   THE SOVIET ECONOMIC CRISIS: PROSPECTS FOR THE MILITARY AND THE CONSUMER by David Fewtrell.
            Winter 1983.
No. 187.   SOVIET THEATRE NUCLEAR FORCES: PART I: DEVELOPMENT OF DOCTRINE AND OBJECTIVES by Stephen
            M. Meyer. Winter 1983/4.
No. 188.   SOVIET THEATRE NUCLEAR FORCES: PART II: CAPABILITIES AND IMPLICATIONS by Stephen M. Meyer.
            Winter 1983/4.
No. 189.   THE CONDUCT OF EAST–WEST RELATIONS IN THE 1980s: PART I: Papers from the IISS 25th Annual
            Conference. Spring 1984.
No. 190.   THE CONDUCT OF EAST–WEST RELATIONS IN THE 1980s: PART II: Papers from the IISS 25th Annual
            Conference. Summer 1984.
No. 191.   THE CONDUCT OF EAST–WEST RELATIONS IN THE 1980s: PART III: Papers from the IISS 25th Annual
            Conference. Summer 1984.
No. 192.   WESTERN SECURITY AND ECONOMIC STRATEGY TOWARDS THE EAST by David Buchan. Autumn 1984.
No. 193.   DETERRENCE IN THE 1980s: PART II: THE ROLE OF CONVENTIONAL AIR POWER by Lt-Col. D. J. Alberts,
            USAF. Winter 1984.
No. 194.   FRANCE'S DETERRENT POSTURE AND SECURITY IN EUROPE: PART I: CAPABILITIES AND DOCTRINE by
            David S. Yost. Winter 1984/85.
No. 195.   FRANCE'S DETERRENT POSTURE AND SECURITY IN EUROPE: PART II: STRATEGIC AND ARMS CONTROL
            IMPLICATIONS by David S. Yost. Winter 1984/85.
No. 196.   INTERVENTION AND REGIONAL SECURITY by Neil Macfarlane. Spring 1985.
No. 197.   NEW TECHNOLOGY AND WESTERN SECURITY POLICY: PART I: Papers from the IISS 26th Annual
            Conference. Summer 1984.
No. 198.   NEW TECHNOLOGY AND WESTERN SECURITY POLICY: PART II: Papers from the IISS 26th Annual
            Conference. Summer 1984.
No. 199.   NEW TECHNOLOGY AND WESTERN SECURITY POLICY: PART III: Papers from the IISS 26th Annual
            Conference. Summer 1984.

Discount rates are available for bulk orders of 11 or more Papers of the same title.